# *Enhance YOUR Mentoring Relationship & Benefits*

## *While Preventing Common Failures*

**William A. Gray, *PhD***

***President of Mentoring Solutions***

*__Enhance YOUR Mentoring Relationship & Benefits
While Preventing Common Failures__*



Email: wgray@mentoring-solutions.com
Website: www.mentoring-solutions.com

*****

**Credits**
Photo: Alex Powell (Pexels)
Cover design: Marilynne Miles Gray
Paint Pad

**Other Books**
*Mentoring, Skill Coaching & Knowledge Solutions: Different Resolutions for Different
Challenges* (2022)
*Mentoring: Aid to Excellence in Education, the Family and Community Vol. 1* (edited
with M.M. Gray)
*Mentoring: Aid to Excellence in Career Development, Business and the Professions Vol.
2* (edited with M.M. Gray)
*Mentoring: A Comprehensive Annotated Bibliography* (with Marilynne Miles Gray)
*Why Become a Christian? A Spiritual Memoir.*
*God Nods on His Story About Me* (2022)
*God Nods on True Love* (2021)
*Learning By Doing: Developing Teaching Skills* (with Brian Gerard, Addison-Wesley)
*Understanding Yourself And Others* (with Brian Gerard, Harper & Row)

*****

# ENDORSEMENTS

My introduction to Bill Gray started in the early 1990s, when **CSX Transportation** started its Associate Development Program (ADP). This began when CEO Pete Carpenter sanctioned this mentoring program so CSX would become more competitive, serve customers better, and increase profitability. CSX hired Bill Gray to conduct his Mentoring for Results Partner Training for CSX personnel at all levels – in management and the union – to break down existing departmental silos. From 1992-2000, Bill encouraged mentoring partners in different functions (e.g., sales and finance) to engage in reciprocal mentoring to break down silo thinking and gain a better appreciation of each other's contributions to the overall company.

After the first eight years, I statistically analyzed all the data from about 300 participants and found that the mentors and proteges who reported the most benefits had been in long-distance relationships (not living or working in the same state). This outcome occurred because Dr. Gray taught partners to create a Mentoring Action Plan during partner training and then use this to schedule meetings and be prepared for them. The long-distance partners did this better than same-location partners.

After 2000, I took over from Bill and conducted his Mentoring for Results Partner Training for CSX – even after I started my own company. I know from 18 years experience as a coordinator and trainer that virtual strangers (who have been matched as partners) feel so comfortable that mentoring actually occurs during partner training. Partners compare protege needs and mentor expertise after answering the Protege Needs Inventory. Partners discuss difficult challenges using Bill's 6-Step Mentoring Process – and then plan how to address this using a Mentoring Action Plan. Partners learn how to use four Mentoring Styles for giving/receiving assistance, after answering Bill's Mentoring Style Indicator.

Even during two recessions, Mentoring for Results Partner Training has continued to take place because it produces *Mentoring Relationships that Produce Results!*

> ~**Dr. Doug Klippel**, former Mentoring Coordinator at CSX and current President of
> People Development Partners (http://www.peopledevpartners.com)

William Gray has produced an epic work on formalized mentoring relationships that work. Bill's work is significant in breaking new ground for understanding the importance of the journey for both the mentor and protege to succeed. Equally important are the tools provided to guide both parties. These tools are like road-signs or directions on a GPS. They guide you to the right destination with the fewest delays. Bill is responsible for my personal success as a mentor, at two organizations (**Air National Guard** and **Defense Supply Center Columbus**) where I helped introduce the formalized mentoring program concept.

> ~**John Murphy**, Retired Lieutenant Colonel USAF, and former Change Manager,
> Defense Supply Center Columbus, Ohio.

When I was **Director of Human Resources for Eastman Kodak**, I was responsible for orienting newly hired researchers into our research labs. They had doctorates from top universities. Because of our reorganization, they had to do applied research for a Business Unit, usually on a team. Previously, they mostly did pure research on their own projects, working alone. To orient them to our new way of doing research, we tried putting them beside veteran researchers in the lab – to receive informal mentoring when needed – but this didn't work. So, I contacted Bill Gray to help us plan and implement a formalized Mentoring Program. To get high-level support, we created an assessment of knowledge, attitudes and competencies that new researchers need to learn during their first six months. During the training of mentor-protege partners, partners created an Action Plan for achieving learning outcomes identified by our assessment.

Because the first program worked so well, I contacted Bill again for help with another challenge. Kodak's leaders had decided to enter the digital age, so we hired new researchers with doctorates in electronics, electrical engineering, and related fields. We wanted them to work with our chemistry-oriented researchers on new hybrid projects, such as the laser printer and digital camera. However, they did not work together very well. During collaborative planning of a mentoring program, we decided that Knowledge Exchange was needed so researchers with backgrounds in chemistry and electronics could mutually exchange knowledge about their discipline – without either partner feeling superior or inferior to the other. After partners were matched, Bill trained them to exchange knowledge about major contributions each discipline can make, key concepts, problem-solving strategies, acronyms and jargon, etc. Partners created an Action Plan to schedule what they would do, so they both would be prepared.

Bill has helped many clients plan and implement formalized mentoring programs that produce intended results. His book describes the approach he has used for over 40 years. I know from personal experience that simply encouraging informal mentoring does not produce desired outcomes for proteges, mentors, and their organization.

I can recommend Bill and this book with complete confidence, based on our professional association over the years we worked together on various Eastman Kodak projects.

~**Bob Calman**, former Director of Human Resources for Eastman Kodak.

# CONTENTS



NOTE: Since 1978, I've used the Anglicized word "**protege**" (meaning the "protected one") for these reasons:

(1) "protege" is of French origin, where "le protégé" (male) and "la protégée" (female) indicate gender;

(2) It is awkward using the two French versions when writing in English;

(3) "protege" has been used longer than "mentee" or "mentoree" or any other word, to designate the recipient of mentoring;

(4) beginning in 1984, I copyrighted over 20 customized mentoring materials that use the word "protege";

(5) over 150 clients have hired me to provide our *Mentoring for Results Training* for Mentor-Protege Partners, using our training materials;

(6) I've trained over 300 Trainers – and over 300 Coordinators – of formalized mentoring programs to use our Partner Training and materials.

# INTRODUCTION

Why you should read

## *Enhance YOUR Mentoring Relationship & Benefits Whlle Preventing Common Failures*.

**MENTORS** and **PROTEGES** [Mentees] will learn *how* to rectify seven common **FAILURES** [described below]. What's learned will enhance all your mentoring relationships, even mentoring your own children.

**Mentoring COORDINATORS** will learn *what* mentoring activities to monitor to enhance success. Such as: satisfying protege needs/goals, equipping and empowering proteges, resolving challenging situations, producing benefits for individual proteges, their mentors and the sponsoring organization.

**CHAMPIONS** of mentoring will understand *why* only an **EXPERT** in *Developing Formalized Mentoring Programs* and in *Training Mentor-Protege Partners* should be hired to prevent seven main **FAILURES**.

What I share with you is based on my training over 20,000 Mentor-Protege Partners in more than 150 organizations where we collaboratively planned and implemented *formalized* mentoring programs. [Read *Mentoring, Skill Coaching & Knowledge Solutions: Different Resolutions for Different Challenges* for client examples from my 45 years of experience.]

Each Chapter ends with **Summarized Tips** for Mentors & Proteges and for Coordinators & Champions.

After answering Questions below, read how to rectify each **FAILURE**.

Failure #1. Mentors do not employ the *right* **Mentoring Styles and behaviors** to help proteges progress through *Levels of Awareness & Competence*.

> o As a protege, have you encountered a situation where you've been **unaware** of what to do AND **unable** to do what's needed? OR **aware** of what to do, BUT **unable** to do what's needed?
>
> o As a mentor, do you know which Mentoring Styles and behaviors will assist your protege to become **aware** of what to do AND **able** to do what's needed?

In Chapter 1, you'll "**Identify Your *Preferred Mentoring Style* and *Level of Awareness & Competence*.**"

Being **aware** of your Preferred Mentoring Style **enables** you to develop *Mentoring Style Flexibility* as a competency – *aware* and *able* to engage in **Situational Mentoring** that is appropriate to each situation.

You'll learn how *Situational Mentoring* helps proteges progress from functioning at an **Unconsciously** or **Consciously Incompetent** Level – to function at a **Consciously Competently** Level to handle challenging situations on their own.

> Failure #2. **Ineffective mentors** do not *equip* AND *empower* proteges.
>
> o As a mentor, do you only *equip* your protege with what you know? Do you *empower* what your protege wants to learn, do and become?
>
> o As a protege, do you mostly want to be *equipped?* Do you mostly want to be *empowered?* Do you need both?

Chapter 2 describes why and how "**Effective Mentors *EQUIP & EMPOWER* Proteges**" by employing appropriate *Mentoring Styles* and associated behaviors.

You'll learn why mentors typically prefer to *equip* proteges with their greater experience and wisdom, but also need to *empower* what proteges want to learn, do and become as well as *empower* contributions they want to make.

You'll learn the **negative consequences** that result when mentors "get stuck" *only* equipping or *only* empowering their proteges.

You'll find out which Mentoring Styles and behaviors to employ to prevent "getting stuck."

> Failure #3. **Unsuccessful proteges** "get stuck" wanting a particular kind of mentoring assistance and support.
>
> o As a protege, do you prefer the *mentor **supporting** what you want to do?* OR prefer the *mentor **telling** you what to do?*
>
> o As a mentor, do you like the protege **relying** *on you?* OR **figuring out** *what to do?*

Chapter 3 describes why and how "**Successful Proteges are *EQUIPPED & EMPOWERED*.**"

You'll learn the ***negative consequences*** that result when proteges "get stuck" wanting *only* equipping or *only* empowering.

You'll learn why **today's proteges** prefer to be *empowered,* but also need *equipping* to be successful.

You'll learn **12 Benefits** my clients reported because proteges were *equipped* with what mentors know and *empowered* to make contributions that benefitted them, their mentors and their organizations.

<table>
<tr><td colspan="2">Failure #4. NO proven mentoring process was used to resolve especially challenging situations (e.g., a complex problem; a personal transformation; a career transition; a dilemma with many options).</td></tr>
<tr><td>o</td><td>As a protege, have you tried to resolve an especially challenging situation on your own – but could not?</td></tr>
<tr><td>o</td><td>As a mentor, do you expect your protege to resolve his/her own challenge? Or, do you resolve the challenge for your protege?</td></tr>
</table>

Chapter 4 describes a "***6-Step Mentoring Process* for Resolving Challenging Situations**" (used by 20,000 mentor-protege partners).

You can read a ***TRANSCRIPT*** of me using this ***6-Step Mentoring Process*** to help my protege (Elaine) make a ***career transition*** that required a ***personal transformation*** in her thinking and actions.

The 4 *Mentoring Styles*/behaviors I employed are clearly labeled and explained so you'll understand how I *equipped* and *empowered* Elaine to progress from being ***Unconsciously Incompetent*** ("I don't have a clue what to do") to become ***Consciously Competent*** ("Now I know what to do because we broke this down into manageable parts").

You'll see our *brainstormed ideas* and resulting ***Mentoring Action Plan*** for achieving her Goal.

<table>
<tr><td colspan="2">Failure #5. Mentor-protege partners are NOT compatible.</td></tr>
<tr><td>o</td><td>As a mentor, did you stop helping an incompatible protege?</td></tr>
<tr><td>o</td><td>As a protege, were you incompatible with your mentor?</td></tr>
</table>

Chapter 5 describes how "**Proven Mentoring Assessments Enhance Mentor-Protege Compatibility & Benefits**" like they did for over 20,000 mentor-protege partners.

You'll answer these Mentoring Assessments to understand how they enhance Partner Compatibility – and the matching of "best-fit" Partners:

> *Mentoring Style Indicator*.

> *Protege Needs Inventory*.

> *General Style of Functioning Indicator*.

> My ***ONE-DAY Partner Matching Process*** saves hundreds of hours and matches ***best-fit*** mentor-protege partners.

<table>
<tr><td colspan="1">Failure #6. Informal "do-your-own-thing" mentoring seldom "happens" when a protege most needs mentor assistance.</td></tr>
<tr><td>o As a protege, did you receive informal mentoring when you most needed it?</td></tr>
<tr><td>o As a mentor, did you provide informal mentoring when most needed?</td></tr>
</table>

Chapter 6 describes how and why *"**Formalized** Mentoring Satisfies Protege Needs better than **Informal** Mentoring."*

You'll learn how 10 distinctive differences of *formalized* mentoring overcome the shortcomings of *informal* mentoring.

You'll find out essential components of *formalized* mentoring programs, which are lacking in *informal* mentoring.

<table>
<tr><td colspan="1">Failure #7. Informal mentoring relationships often end badly.</td></tr>
<tr><td>o As a protege, have you experienced a "power struggle" before your informal mentor would let you leave? Or, have you wanted to stay when the mentor wanted you to leave?</td></tr>
<tr><td>o As an informal mentor, did you encourage your protege to go? Or, did you pressure your protege to stay?</td></tr>
</table>

Chapter 7 explains how to employ what you've learned in Chapters 1-6:

You'll understand why and how *informal* mentoring often ends badly.

You'll understand why and how *formalized* mentoring ends well, by reading actual examples.

After benefitting from *formalized* mentoring, proteges typically want to mentor others like they were mentored. My poem – ***Mentor Me*** – describes this.

You'll learn how to ***Manage Mentoring*** – like I did by guiding my mentor to employ the *6-Step Mentoring Process* and provide *Situational Mentoring* – to help me ***transition*** from salaried professor to revenue-generating business owner, and make necessary ***transformations*** in my thinking and actions.

Proteges will learn how to ***Manage Mentoring*** so you receive the *equipping* and *empowering* you need to satisfy important Needs/Goals.

# Bottom Line

Reading this book and applying what you learn will ***Enhance YOUR Mentoring Relationship & Benefits*** – as it has for over 20,000 mentor-protege partners, whom I've trained. Intended Benefits have resulted for individual proteges and their mentors and for their organizations. And will result for you, too!

---

Another book describes 45 years of my work/passion:

### *Mentoring, Skill Coaching & Knowledge Solutions: Different Resolutions for Different Challenges*

✓ **Mentor grade 4-12 Youth** so they learn about careers that match their talents and aspirations. We discovered essential components for creating a **Talent / Workforce Development Pipeline** (comprised of Youth + Undergrad-mentors + STEM Professionals).

✓ **Mentor college students** to succeed academically and **mentor college interns/co-ops** so they learn about the sponsoring company and hire on. This saves recruiting dollars.

✓ **Mentor new hires** to feel welcome, get up to speed faster, begin preparing for career development, and remain with the company; reducing turnover pays for such mentoring.

✓ **Mentor career exploration** so the right career path is taken for the right reasons. (e.g., you don't want unprepared "techies" take the managerial path when they should not).

✓ **Mentor career expansion** to reduce costly turnover when promotion isn't possible.

✓ **Mentor career development** so proteges are properly prepared and will be successful.

✓ **Mentor leaders for succession planning** to support talent development courses and to gain wisdom and practical know-how from C-level Officers to "run" the organization.

✓ **Mentor/coach improved Person-Job Fit** so one's typical style of functioning better matches what the job or position requires. This improves performance and reduces turnover.

✓ **Mentor the diversified workforce** so unique talents and creativity are empowered.

---

######

# Chapter 1

## Identify Your *Preferred Mentoring Style &*
## *Level of Awareness & Competence*

Chapter 1 describes Mentoring Activities that typically occur when I conduct ***Mentoring for Results Partner Training*** (for over 20,000 Mentor-Protege Partners thus far):

> ➢ Partners answer the *Mentoring Style Indicator* to identify their Preferred Mentoring Styles.

> ➢ Partners discuss "NOT getting stuck" on a Preferred Mentoring Style. [Chapters 2&3 describe how to develop a "dynamic" relationship.]

> ➢ Partners identify *Level of Awareness & Competence.*

### Identify Your Preferred Mentoring Style

Since 1980, different clients have helped us to identify Mentoring Situations that are commonly encountered by a particular group of proteges. This enabled us to create different versions of the ***Mentoring Style Indicator*** (*MSI*) for different kinds of proteges, mentors and situations:

o For **business and government situations**, I developed a *MSI* for: orienting new hires, aiding career development, developing leaders, sales training, health care professionals, and for entrepreneurs. Plus a Generic Version.

o For **education situations**, I developed a *MSI* for: inducting new teachers, preparing new school administrators, mentoring youth, helping freshmen stay in college, and for developing college/university faculty.

Below, are six ***MSI* Situations** from six versions of the *MSI*, for you to answer to find out your **Preferred Mentoring Style** as a PROTEGE or as a MENTOR.

### Directions for each Situation: as a **PROTEGE** or **MENTOR**

1) To the **left** of each statement, rank order (4,3,2,1) the help you would prefer to **receive** as a Protege or **provide** as a Mentor.

2) Record 4 as your top choice and 1 as your lowest choice.

3) Record 2 or 3 as "in between" choices for each Situation.

## Situation 1.
## [From *MSI for New Hires*]

**Situation:** Protege successfully completed two co-op experiences in different divisions (and locations) of a large company before being offered employment as a new hire. As a co-op student, Protege was perceived as a self-reliant "individualist" who always worked hard to produce excellent results that exceeded expectations. Protege did not pay any attention to "fitting in" with the company's image, unwritten rules and norms. Now, as a new hire with potential long-range career possibilities, Protege is suddenly concerned about the dilemma of how to "fit in" while "maintaining personal individuality." How might a mentor help?

- o S1: Mentor gives advice for Protege to follow.
- o S2: Mentor offers suggestions for Protege to consider, based on greater experience.
- o S3: Mentor and Protege discuss this dilemma and jointly plan how to resolve it.
- o S4: Mentor is non-judgmental while Protege expresses ideas for resolving this dilemma.

## Situation 2.
## [From *MSI for Career Development*]

**Situation:** Protege's analytic style – coupled with brilliant technical expertise – has made the Protege successful doing Research and Development. Now, Protege has been become project manager of an R&D project whose success is key to the organization's profitability and stock market performance. Protege is experiencing difficulty getting the interdepartmental team to work together smoothly, and is unaware of essential "people skills" needed to do this. Protege views this "stormy period" as inevitable, and is reluctant to seek out help. How might a Mentor help?

- o S1: Mentor arranges for Protege to receive coaching to develop needed people skills.
- o S2: Mentor persuades Protege that employing good "people skills" is now more important than providing technical expertise.
- o S3: Mentor and Protege agree on when to provide technical expertise and when to use "people skills."
- o S4: Mentor listens and summarizes protege's concerns and ideas for handling this situation.

## Situation 3.
## [From *MSI for Developing Leaders*]

**Situation:** Protege has managed the largest department very well – overseeing day-to-day operations, motivating and coaching staff to improve performance, and surpassing all expectations for innovation and productivity. This has earned a promotion to Leader for Corporate Innovation in a company where departments have traditionally functioned as "silos" that do not communicate with other departments. As the new Innovation Leader, Protege is having difficulty (a) providing visionary ideas and motivation needed for creativity and (b) getting interdepartmental cooperation to work on new innovative products. How might a mentor help?

- o S1: Mentor self-discloses a personal transformation that resulted in being an effective, visionary leader.

- o S2: Mentor asks probing questions that prompt Protege to recall things done in the past that can be used to overcome both current difficulties.

- o S3: Mentor and Protege brainstorm creative ideas for overcoming both difficulties.

- o S4: Mentor paraphrases (reflects back) Protege's ideas for increasing innovation and interdepartmental cooperation.

## Situation 4.
## [From *MSI for Sales Training and Development*]

**Situation:** Protege does not want to be viewed as the proverbial "pushy and aggressive" sales person. Protege joined the company because its high-quality products "sell themselves." Protege is being trained to use "promotions" and "add-on sales techniques" to meet sales quotas. Protege believes this is too much like a "hard sell" approach and feels uncomfortable doing these things. How might a mentor help?

- o S1: Mentor describes how other sales personnel are using these new techniques to meet sales quotas.

- o S2: Mentor coaches Protege and demonstrates how these new sales techniques are helpful in meeting customer needs.

- o S3: Mentor and Protege together develop a plan for using "promotions" and "add-on sales techniques."

- o S4: Mentor encourages Protege to propose actions that will resolve this situation to everyone's satisfaction.

## Situation 5.
## [From *MSI for Health Care Professionals*]

**Situation:** Protege recently became Lead Physician in a very busy department that handles the most complex patient problems. This requires a much higher level of problem-solving capability and time management than where Protege previously worked. Protege is reluctant to acknowledge this or seek assistance, because of a tendency to "figure out what to do." Protege believes professionals should do this instead of admitting weakness by requesting help. Unless assistance is sought and heeded, major problems will result. How might a mentor help?

- o S1: Mentor explains proven problem-solving techniques and a time management strategy.
- o S2: Mentor asks leading questions so Protege realizes the negative consequences that will result unless assistance is requested immediately.
- o S3: Mentor and Protege dialogue about the "pros" and "cons" of seeking help versus "figuring out what to do."
- o S4: Mentor serves as a sounding board for Protege's concerns and ideas.

## Situation 6.
## [From *MSI for Generic Issues*]

**Situation:** Protege enjoys the "creative process" – starting new projects, initiating change – much more than carrying out tasks necessary for completing what has been started. Lately, Protege has started so many new things at work and at home that nothing is being completed – except by other people who are now resenting Protege's "impulsiveness." To rectify this situation and win back admiration, Protege must shift focus from "being creative" to "completing tasks." How might a mentor help?

- o S1: Mentor teaches Protege task-oriented techniques for completing what is started.
- o S2: Mentor confronts Protege's impulsiveness to start something new so often, without completing what has already been started.
- o S3: Mentor and Protege decide when it is appropriate to "be creative" and "complete tasks."
- o S4: Mentor clarifies Protege's concerns and ideas for rectifying this situation to regain admiration.

## <u>Calculate your Preferred Mentoring Style:</u>

1) For each Situation above, write down the **RANK** (4,3,2,1) you gave to each Style.

2) In each Column, add up your scores to calculate your **Total Score** for each Style.

3) **Highest Total Score**(s) indicate *your* Preferred Mentoring Style (could be a single Style, or 2 or more Styles).

| Situation | S1 = Informational Style | S2 = Guiding Style | S3 = Collaborative Style | S4 = Confirming Style |
|---|---|---|---|---|
| 1 | | | | |
| 2 | | | | |
| 3 | | | | |
| 4 | | | | |
| 5 | | | | |
| 6 | | | | |
| **Total Score** | | | | |

## <u>Directions:</u>

4) Add the **4 Total Scores** in the bottom Row. If this Grand Total is not "**60**," you have made a mistake Ranking the 4 kinds of mentoring assistance or you made a mistake adding numbers in each Column above.

5) When the **Grand Total=60**, read the Interpretation of your Preferred Mentoring Style on the next pages.

6) Then, *GRAPH* your Preferred Mentoring Style and your partner's also.

### Graph Your Preferred Mentoring Style PROFILE as PROTEGE or MENTOR

## <u>Directions:</u>

1) In the top graph below, circle your scores as a Protege.

2) In the bottom graph, circle your scores as a Mentor.

3) Read an *Interpretation of Your Preferred Mentoring Profile.*

| Mentoring Style | Protege's Mentoring Style Preferences | | |
| --- | --- | --- | --- |
| | Weak | Moderate | Strong |
| S1- Informational | 6 7 8 9 10 11 | 12 13 14 15 16 17 18 | 19 20 21 22 23 24 |
| S2- Guiding | 6 7 8 9 10 11 | 12 13 14 15 16 17 18 | 19 20 21 22 23 24 |
| S3- Collaborative | 6 7 8 9 10 11 | 12 13 14 15 16 17 18 | 19 20 21 22 23 24 |
| S4- Confirming | 6 7 8 9 10 11 | 12 13 14 15 16 17 18 | 19 20 21 22 23 24 |

| Mentoring Style | Mentor's Mentoring Style Preferences | | |
| --- | --- | --- | --- |
| | Weak | Moderate | Strong |
| S1- Informational | 6 7 8 9 10 11 | 12 13 14 15 16 17 18 | 19 20 21 22 23 24 |
| S2- Guiding | 6 7 8 9 10 11 | 12 13 14 15 16 17 18 | 19 20 21 22 23 24 |
| S3- Collaborative | 6 7 8 9 10 11 | 12 13 14 15 16 17 18 | 19 20 21 22 23 24 |
| S4- Confirming | 6 7 8 9 10 11 | 12 13 14 15 16 17 18 | 19 20 21 22 23 24 |

## Overview of *Equipping & Empowering*
### [Chapters 2&3 describe this fully]

The ***Informational*** and ***Guiding*** Mentoring Styles ***EQUIP*** proteges with what the mentor knows. *Equipping* enables proteges to function successfully in situations where the protege is ***unaware*** of what to do AND ***unable*** to do what's needed. Or, is ***aware*** BUT ***unable*** to function successfully

The ***Collaborative*** and ***Confirming*** Mentoring Styles ***EMPOWER*** what proteges want to learn, do and become. *Empowering* enables proteges to make contributions to the organization – because proteges are ***aware*** AND ***able*** to do what's needed.

Keep this in mind as you continue reading.

## Read Interpretation of
## Your Preferred Mentoring Style PROFILE

There are 3 **PROFILES** of Preferred Mentoring Style:
- ➢ ***Single Dominant Style Profile*** indicated by *only one* Score of 19 or more (Strong Preference in the graph).
- ➢ ***Mixed Style Profile*** comprised of 2 or 3 Single Styles (indicated by 2 or 3 Scores of 19 or more).
- ➢ ***Balanced Style Profile*** where all four Styles have Scores between 12 to 18 (Moderate range in the graph).

Because most people prefer a ***Mixed Style*** – and the ***Balanced Style*** is an ideal to aim for – I've described these PROFILES below. [In the actual ***MSI***, you can read a detailed description of each Single Style.]

### Mixed Informational-Guiding Mentoring Style
### (*EQUIP* proteges with Style 1/2 Combination  or "M+Mp")

These mentors like to play a leading, directing, structuring role in *equipping* proteges to succeed. These proteges like to be equipped by accessing and utilizing mentor-provided expertise and wisdom. Overly using Style 1/2 with dependent-prone proteges reinforces their dependency on what the mentor provides. Inappropriately using this Style 1/2 combination with more mature, confident, self-reliant, and capable proteges will usually produce a power struggle as these proteges resist mentor domination and strive for autonomy.

### Mixed Collaborative-Confirming Style
### (*EMPOWER* proteges with Style 3/4 Combination  or "MP+mP")

These mentors *empower* proteges to play a major role in making decisions and solving problems; these proteges welcome this responsibility. However, using this Style 3/4 combination inappropriately with proteges who really do not know how to solve their own problems may contribute to their failing in a crucial situation, with long-term disastrous consequences.

### Mixed Guiding-Collaborative Mentoring Style
### (Style 2/3 Combination  or "Mp+MP")

This Mentoring Style combination indicates mentor preference to exert a major influence on proteges while interacting with them rather than transmitting information via a one-way communication. This Style 2/3 combination is appropriate for proteges who have sufficient maturity, experience and expertise to apply useful mentor suggestions and to make joint decisions and action plans. Using a Collaborative Style more than a Guiding Style *empowers* protege progress towards greater competence and autonomous functioning.

### Mixed Informational-Guiding-Collaborative Style
### (Style 1/2/3 Combination  or "M+Mp+MP")

Mentors who prefer a Style 1/2/3 combination want to have an active, major influence on proteges' development instead of letting them sink or swim. Proteges who prefer this Style welcome such mentoring, but must guard against becoming dependent on it.

### Mixed Guiding-Collaborative-Confirming Style
### (Style 2/3/4 Combination  or "Mp+MP+mP")

This Style 2/3/4 combination indicates a preference for interacting with proteges rather than unilaterally prescribing/arranging what they should do (Style 1). This Style combination is not appropriate for proteges who need a lot of initial external prescribed strategy for solving urgent problems quickly.

**BALANCED Mentoring Style**
**(Styles 1/2/3/4 Equally Preferred or "M+Mp+MP+mP")**

These mentors like to **style-shift** to employ maximal *Mentoring Style Flexibility* when providing help; these proteges welcome such versatility and seek it out to match their situational needs and capability. In sum, all four mentoring styles are appropriately preferred and employed, as needed. This is an *ideal to develop*.

# How to Enhance
# Your Mentor-Protege Relationship

1) Ask your potential or actual partner to answer the *MSI Situations* above (as PROTEGE, if you are the mentor; as MENTOR, if you are the protege).

2) Your partner should **Calculate** scores (like you did).

3) **Graph** your partner's scores to identify his/her **Profile**.

4) **Compare** both Profiles.

5) Read and discuss **Interpretations** of both Profiles, then **Answer these Questions:**

   o   Are both Profiles similar or different? Why?
   o   Which Profile most prefers Equipping? Empowering? Why?
   o   As a Mentor, would you clash with you as a Protege?

#####

After identifying your Preferred Mentoring Style, you're ready to find out *when* to employ different Mentoring Styles and associated behaviors – and *why* this is important for *Enhancing Your Mentoring Relationship & Benefits*:

> The *Informative* and *Guiding* Mentoring Styles are needed when proteges are functioning at the two lowest *Levels of Awareness & Competence*.

> The *Collaborative* and *Confirming* Mentoring Styles are appropriate when the protege is functioning at higher *Levels*.

# Identify *Level of Awareness & Competence*

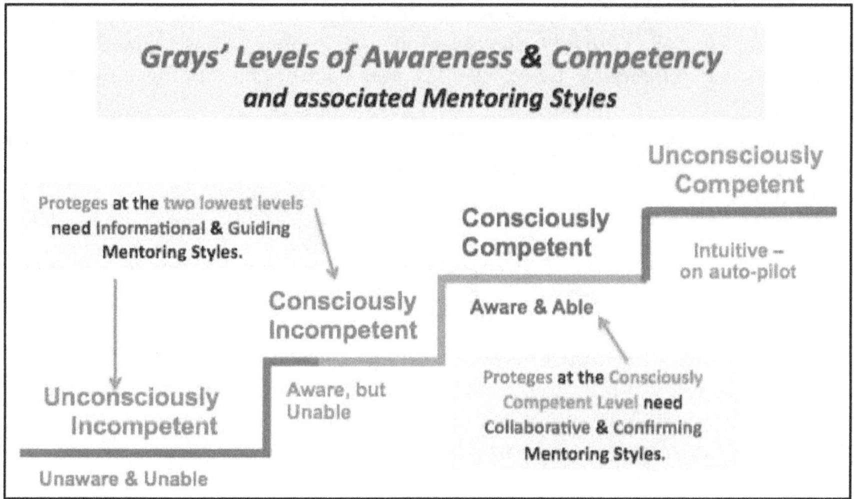


Here is an overview of the 4 *Levels of Awareness and Competence*:

- o **Unconsciously Incompetent** (Level 1) – *unaware* of what to do in a particular situation and *unable* to do what's needed (lacks needed competence).

- o **Consciously Incompetent** (Level 2) – *aware* of what to do, but still *unable* (lacks needed competence).

- o **Consciously Competent** (Level 3) – *aware* of what to do and *able* to function successfully.

- o **Unconsciously Competent** (Level 4) – *unaware* of what you do while being *able* to function "intuitively" – on "automatic pilot" – because of many years of experience developing a particular area of expertise.

**PROTEGES:** Have you encountered a challenging situation where you were functioning at either of the two lowest levels? Did you resolve this situation successfully? Why or why not?

**MENTORS:** Did you ever have a protege who was functioning at either of the two lowest levels? Did you help this protege resolve this situation successfully? Why or why not?

**Here is what works:**

Being ***aware*** of your Preferred Mentoring Style ***enables*** mentoring partners to employ *Mentoring Style Flexibility – aware* and *able* to engage in *Situational Mentoring* that is appropriate to each situation.

Effective mentors *equip* proteges to progress from functioning at an ***Unconsciously*** or ***Consciously*** *Incompetent* Level – to function at a ***Consciously Competently*** Level so they can handle challenging situations on their own.

When proteges function at the ***Consciously Competently*** Level  – *aware* and *able* – effective mentors *empower* them to make contributions that benefit their organizations.

## Importance of
### *Levels of Awareness & Competence*

I first discovered the lowest three *Levels of Awareness & Competence* while working with **Eastman Kodak** in the late-1980s. I discovered the highest Level while working with **Norwest Bank** (now called Wells Fargo) in the early 1990s. Here is why knowing *Level of Awareness & Competence* is important:

**At Eastman Kodak – proteges progressed from *Unconsciously Incompetent* to *Consciously Competent*:**

Before hiring me, Kodak had placed experienced researchers (who agreed to be *informal* mentors) to work beside new researchers. No actual mentor-protege matching was done, nor was training provided. Kodak simply expected these new hires would request needed assistance from more experienced near-by colleagues, when they needed this.

But, new researchers did not request *informal* mentoring. Why not? These newly hired PhD professionals believed they should already know what to do or be able to figure out what to do – because "we're PhD professionals." Until I was told this, I didn't know this is a common mindset of many highly educated professionals.

I realized these newly hired professionals were functioning at the two lowest *Levels of Awareness & Competence*

Because of a *major restructuring* in Kodak's Research Labs, these new researchers were required to make a **transition** in how they worked and make an **inner transformation** in how they think.

- They could not do pure research of personal interest while working on their own.
- Now, they were required to do *applied* research that met Business Unit needs associated with new product development – and they had to work on an interdisciplinary *team*.

When Bob Calman (mentoring coordinator) and I realized the mindset of these new PhD professionals (not to seek help):

➢ We created an **Orientation Mentoring Program** so *formalized* mentoring would be systematically provided

➢ We made asking for help acceptable by creating a ***Protege Needs Inventory***. Each protege quickly indicated the most important Needs to focus on and satisfy.

➢ *Formalized* mentoring systematically assisted these new hires to progress from the two lowest *Levels of Awareness & Competence* to function at the ***Consciously Competent Level*** in the restructured Research Labs.


**At Norwest Bank – mentors stopped being *Unconsciously Competent* to function *Consciously Competent*:**

A group of mentors objected to being *trained* to provide *formalizing* mentoring because they were functioning at the ***Unconsciously Competent Level*** after providing *informal* mentoring for many years. These resistant mentors said:

"I know all about mentoring."

"I won't learn anything new."

"Waste of my valuable time."

These mentors needed to function at a lower level – the ***Consciously Competent Level*** – to effectively help their proteges. They could not do this "intuitively" at the higher ***Unconsciously Competent Level.***


Here's the story:


Rick Beresford, Director of Norwest's Human Resources Department, realized that new MBAs needed systematic assistance to orient them into the organization. They came to Norwest very idealistic, and quickly departed when their expectations were not met. So, a steering committee and I designed a *formalized* mentoring program. Rick publicized program expectations, selected applicants, and matched mentor-protege partners.

Several weeks before I was scheduled to train mentor-protege partners, Rick told me that half of the mentors wanted to be excused from the training session. This one-day session was intended to teach mentoring partners how to work together and be productive – impossible without the mentors.

So, I flew to Minneapolis a day early to walk all the mentors through the next day's Partner Training activities and explain the difference between the *informal* mentoring they were accustomed to providing and the more *formalized* mentoring they had volunteered to provide.

This did not convince the resistant mentors. With Rick's backing, I told them that because the training was designed for partners, if they decided not to attend, their protege partners could not attend, and they must phone their proteges that night and explain why their proteges could not attend tomorrow – and tell their protege he/she could not participate in the Mentoring Program.

Everyone showed up for Partner Training – and the 'resistant' mentors individually told me how he/she benefitted from participating:

"It would have taken at least 6 months to do with my partner what we did today."

"Discussing our *Preferred Mentoring Styles* today will prevent us from 'getting stuck'."

"Until today, I hadn't created a *Mentoring Action Plan* to achieve protege goals."

"I had never used a *Protege Needs Inventory* to pin point exactly what we needed to focus on."

"We entered your Partner Training as strangers, but now know lots about one another ... we like what we've learned."

"I'm so glad I participated today – you're right, we both had to be here."

## Insights About Newer Hires
### [can be veterans new to the organization]

**Brand new hires** [0-4 months on the job] don't really know their skill and knowledge *gap*s, and therefore, don't know exactly what help to request. Mostly, they are functioning at the ***Unconsciously Incompetent*** level - *unaware* of what's important to know and *unable* to perform effectively. They lack both knowledge and ability. They need *equipping* to get up to speed and feel welcomed.

**Recent hires** [4-8 months on the job] are starting to function at the ***Consciously Incompetent*** level - they are becoming *aware* of what's important to know and do, but are still *unable* to perform fully competently. They need *equipping* to become fully competent on the job plus *empowering* to make contributions to the organization.

---

***Full Competency*** is comprised of four components:
- ✓ Conceptual knowledge and understanding what to do.
- ✓ Having a "can do" positive attitude/motivation.
- ✓ Having requisite skill mastery (being *able*).
- ✓ Having *awareness* needed to make situational adjustments.

---

## Formalized Mentoring of Newer Hires

**Orientation Mentoring Programs** are started to assist newer hires "learn the ropes" and "get up to speed" because these proteges are functioning at the *two lowest **Levels of Awareness & Competency*** due to their *lack* of real world experience and practical know-how. A properly designed and implemented Program can produce multiple benefits, such as:

➢ Recruit new hires who want formalized mentoring.

➢ Help new hires make the *transition* from being students to becoming professionals – and make needed *personal transformations* (thinking, attitudes, behaviors, habits) that this requires.

➢ Shorten the time needed to "get up to speed" on their new jobs – by developing and employing needed competencies (connecting "head knowledge" with "practical know-how").

➢ "Learn the ropes": the unwritten rules, cultural norms, and expectations.

➢ Assimilate into the organization so they feel welcomed and gain a sense of *belonging* – while maintaining their uniqueness/diversity.

➢ Progress from functioning at an *Unconsciously* or *Consciously Incompetent* Level of Awareness & Competency to function at the *Consciously Competent* Level.

➢ Become *equipped* to function more competently and *empowered* to make unique contributions.

➢ Reduce turnover of newer hires who might want to leave – by benefitting in the ways mentioned above.

## Formalized Mentoring for Career Development

Organizations start three types of *formalized* mentoring programs to aid Career Development in different ways:

**Career *Expansion* Mentoring Programs** can be used when vertical promotion isn't possible – to do something personally interesting and challenging. These creative contributions can prevent organizational stagnation. Such programs also reduce turnover.

**Career *Exploration* Mentoring Programs** can be used when promotions are possible *and* the best career path option must be chosen. Best for the individual because professional talents match what the new position requires. Best for the organization because the right person is in the right position and can perform required functions appropriately.

**Career *Development* Mentoring Programs** develop specific aspects of individuals to prepare them to *transition* into another position – a vertical transition to a higher position in the organizational hierarchy (e.g., supervisor to manager; manager to leader) or a lateral move (e.g., technical position to managerial position; doctor to clinic manager). Usually requires a presonal *transformation* in one's thinking and actions.

## Formalized Mentoring of Future Leaders & Executives

Formalized mentoring equips and empowers talented individuals to make *transformations* in thinking and acting required to *transition* from performing managerial functions to perform leadership functions:

| Managerial Functions | Leader Functions |
|---|---|
| Administers | Innovates |
| Has short-range view | Has long-range view |
| Asks *How* to do tasks | Asks *What* emerging tasks need to be done |
| Asks *When* to do tasks | Asks *Why* do this |
| Watches bottom line | Watches horizon |
| Maintains status quo | Challenges status quo |
| ~ Warren Bennis, *Leadership in the 21st Century* (1989) | |

To summarize:

- ❖ Managers typically focus on overseeing day-to-day operations, ensuring that their direct reports have the necessary resources and competencies to adequately do their jobs.

- ❖ Leaders must see the big picture to anticipate *new* directions, products, services, markets, and the organizational changes they must lead.

**Summarized Tips for Mentors:**
1. Employ your *least preferred* Mentoring Styles *more* – to develop Mentoring Style Flexibility (*Situational Mentoring*) that a protege needs.
2. When your protege is functioning at Level 1 or 2 of *Awareness and Competence*, employ *Informational* and/or *Guiding* Mentoring Styles to equip this protege to progress to Level 3 – to be *Consciously Competent* in handling a particular situation.

**Summarized Tips for Proteges:**
1. Request those Mentoring Styles/behaviors you *least prefer* to receive.
2. Identify a situation where you are functioning at Level 1 or 2 of *Awareness and Competence*, and then identify a mentor who can employ *Informational* and/or *Guiding* Mentoring Styles to help you reach Level 3 – to be *Consciously Competent* in handling this situation.

**Summarized Tips for Coordinators & Champions:**
1. Have mentor-protege partners (independently of one another) answer the *Mentoring Style Indicator*, to identify the Mentoring Style each mentor prefers to provide and each protege prefers to receive. Have partners compare their Preferred Mentoring Styles.

2. Teach those mentoring behaviors that are least preferred, and thus not employed very often.
3. Match a mentor with a protege who needs equipping (and empowering) to reach the *Consciously Competent Level* to handle a particular situation. Make sure appropriate Mentoring Styles and behaviors are employed.

#####

# Chapter 2

## Effective Mentors
## *EQUIP* & *EMPOWER* Proteges

**Chapter 2 describes:**

> ➢ Negative consequences that result when well-meaning mentors "get stuck":
>
>> o   only *equipping* proteges with what mentors know.
>>
>> o   only *empowering* what proteges want to learn, do and become.
>
> ➢ Why a "dynamic relationship" is necessary for success.
>
> ➢ How 2 ***Mentoring Styles*** and associated behaviors *equip* proteges.
>
> ➢ How 2 ***Mentoring Styles*** and associated behaviors *empower* proteges.

You'll also learn:

- Why mentors typically prefer to *equip* proteges with their greater experience and wisdom, but also need to *empower* proteges.

- Why today's proteges prefer to be *empowered*, but need both *equipping* and *empowering* to become successful. [Examples described in Chapter 3.]

### My R&D Discoveries

In 1978, when I started creating mentor-protege partnerships, no one knew that mentors and proteges needed training – because none is provided for *informal* mentoring partners. Nearly 100% of the literature on mentoring at that time described *informal* mentoring – the kind that just "happens spontaneously" without any formal process for matching mentoring partners or training them.

So, I made a simple "*Announcement*" to request volunteers, matched mentors with proteges without any sound criteria, gave partners a brief pep talk, and sent them on their way – without providing any training.

No wonder results were mixed (both positive and negative). From structured interviews, I discovered that half the relationships were successful because partners developed a "*dynamic*" relationship. But, half the mentor-protege *relationships* failed, and as a result, protege goals were not attained. What went wrong? Mentors and proteges separately reported the same reason: "*Our relationship got stuck.*"

Before writing this chapter, I decided to describe *getting stuck* (what NOT to do), before describing what to DO (engage in *Situational Mentoring*). Knowing what NOT to do will motivate you to avoid the negative consequences this produces – so you'll be even more motivated to engage in *Situational Mentoring*, which develops good relationships that produce more benefits.

### How Mentors "Got Stuck"
### *Equipping* Proteges

According to the proteges, some mentors "got stuck telling" proteges what to do. These mentors continuously provided advice, guidance and wise counsel.

Mentors told me they wanted to **equip** proteges for these reasons:

- ✓ "Imparting what I know validates my experiences."
- ✓ "It's my responsibility to *equip* proteges with what I know."
- ✓ "I've always done this while providing *informal* mentoring."
- ✓ "This is the classic, historical definition of mentoring – to provide advice, guidance and wise counsel."

Proteges initially welcomed such mentoring because it prevented needless mistakes. Unfortunately, these mentors did not recognize when proteges had become more competent and confident, but persisted in *equipping* them with what they knew from greater experience (mostly telling them what to do).

Proteges eventually viewed these mentors as being so *domineering* that they stopped seeking mentor assistance. This eventually caused the relationship to unravel.

### How Mentors "Got Stuck"
### *Empowering* Proteges

Some mentors got stuck **overly *empowering* proteges** to figure out what to do – even when they couldn't. These mentors got stuck being too non-directive because they wanted to *empower* proteges to make independent decisions, initiate appropriate action, figure out how to solve problems, and take more risks. Even when proteges were struggling with a situation and went to their mentors for direction, mentors insisted that proteges handle it on their own.

At this point, the proteges realized that the mentors were not going to provide needed assistance, and stopped seeking any more mentoring.

NOTE: Chapter 3 describes how proteges "got stuck" and 12 benefits that resulted when they did not "get stuck" but engaged in a "dynamic" relationship.

### A "Dynamic" Mentoring Relationship
### Produces Success

In marked contrast to failed "stuck" relationships, mentoring relationships were successful when no one "got stuck" in the ways just described. Successful mentors and proteges found it very difficult to describe their relationship because, instead being stagnant, it continually changed:

- ✓ "Our relationship was dynamic."
- ✓ "We didn't do any one thing all the time."
- ✓ "Mentors provided many different kinds of assistance."
- ✓ "Proteges were receptive to any assistance I provided."

My **Mentor-Protege Relationship Model** illustrates this varied mentor assistance, portrayed as 4 Mentoring Styles and associated mentoring behaviors.

## Gray's Mentor-Protege Relationship Model™

| M ——— Mp ——— MP ——— mP ——— P | | | | |
|---|---|---|---|---|
| **Style 1** **Informational Mentoring Style** Mentor uses 1-way communication to impart information | **Style 2** **Guiding Mentoring Style** Mentor guides 2-way communication during interaction with Protege | **Style 3** **Collaborative Mentoring Style** M&P jointly contribute & interact with no one dominating | **Style 4** **Confirming Mentoring Style** Mentor acknowledges & confirms Protege's ideas & feelings | **Goal is** **Successful Protege** Consciously Competent – aware of what to do & able to do it |
| • Self–discloses<br>• Describes<br>• Teaches<br>• Explains<br>• Arranges help<br>• Praises<br>• Advises<br>• Prescribes<br>√ P is receptive | • Suggests<br>• Persuades<br>• Confronts<br>• Asks Leading Questions<br>• Probes<br>• Coaches<br>√ P responds to M's guidance | • 2-way Dialog<br>• Jointly make decisions & solve problems<br>• Agree on action steps<br>√ P contributes in major ways | • Sounding Board<br>• Clarifies<br>• Paraphrases<br>• Summarizes<br>• Non-threatening<br>• Non-judgmental<br>• Encourages<br>√ P proposes ideas & actions | • Aware<br>• Competent<br>• Self-motivated<br>• Confident<br>• Creative<br>• Problem-solver<br>• Leader, mentor |



In successful relationships, mentors employed different kinds of mentoring behaviors to provide appropriate kinds of assistance, depending on what proteges needed at any given point in time.

And, proteges were *receptive* to the varied assistance provided, and *utilized* this to function successfully and achieve desired goals.

Neither partner "got stuck" in the ways previously described. Relationships stayed *dynamic*, ever-changing, developing in a positive and productive manner, because both *equipping* and *empowering* occurred in a flexible, appropriate manner.

While listening to these mentors and proteges report what occurred in these successful relationships, I began to understand that the 25 mentoring behaviors mentors provided could be grouped into four categories, which I called **Mentoring Styles**.

This discovery led me to conceptualize **Gray's *Situational Mentoring Model***, and to portray the four Mentoring Styles within this Model.

### *Informational* And *Guiding* Mentoring Styles
### *EQUIP* Proteges

Effective mentors *flexibly* employ 14 mentoring behaviors (explained below) to **equip** proteges with wisdom, practical know-how, "tricks of the trade" and other "lessons learned." This occurs when mentors employ the **Informational** and **Guiding** Mentoring Styles.

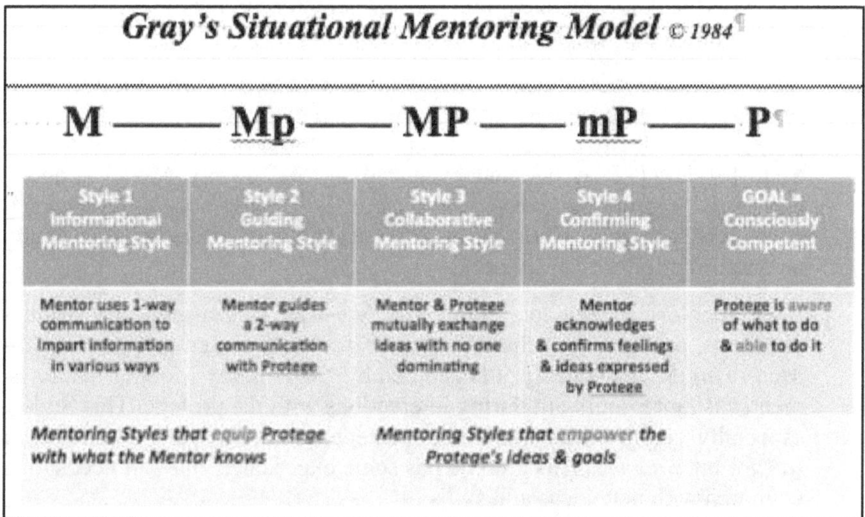


### *Collaborative* And *Confirming* Mentoring Styles
### *EMPOWER* Proteges

Mentors must do more than just *equip* proteges with what they know – so they don't produce clones. Mentors must ***empower*** the protege's uniqueness, creativity, diversity, passions, and goals so the protege becomes a contributor, who adds value to the organization to prevent stagnation.

Effective mentors *flexibly* employ 11 mentoring behaviors to **empower** what proteges want to learn, do, and become as mentors employ the ***Collaborative*** and ***Confirming*** Mentoring Styles.

> Chapter 3 describes important Benefits when proteges are *equipped* and *empowered* – plus actual examples my clients reported.

## How I Discovered *Situational Mentoring* & Its Importance

You might be wondering how I identified four *Mentoring Styles* in the late 1970s, and portrayed them in my *Situational Mentoring Model*.

First, I identified 24 different mentoring behaviors that effective mentors provided.

Second, to make sense of these behaviors, I asked myself: What do particular behaviors have in common? (This step was similar to doing a factor analysis, using statistics to find out what "clusters together" around a common factor).

Third, because I understood how different communication patterns occur between individuals, I realized that certain mentoring behaviors "clustered together" around a particular communication pattern:

o Some mentoring behaviors involved a **one-way communication** of information (giving advice, praise, etc.) imparted from the mentor to the protege without any interaction. I named this the *Informational Mentoring Style* [Style 1]. It is denoted by a capital "**M**" in my Model – and is especially appropriate when the protege is *Unconsciously Incompetent* (*unaware & unable*) – and needs different kinds of information to handle an unfamiliar or critical situation.

o Some mentoring behaviors involved a **two-way communication** (leading questions, probing, etc.) that the mentor guides. I named this the *Guiding Mentoring Style* [Style 2]. It is denoted by "**Mp**" in my Model because the mentor is more dominant during interactions with the protege. This Style is especially appropriate when the protege is *Consciously Incompetent* (*aware* but *unable*). This protege has some experience, but still needs to be equipped with new ideas and skills.

o Some mentoring behaviors involved a **collaborative exchange** of ideas (dialogue, joint decision-making, etc.), with no one dominating. I named this the *Collaborative Mentoring Style* [Style 3]. It is denoted by "**MP**" in my Model – and is especially appropriate when the protege is *Consciously Competent* (*aware & able*). This protege has sufficient experience to contribute during back-and-forth interactions with the mentor.

o Some mentoring behaviors (sounding board, encouragement, etc.) were **confirming** and **supportive** of what the protege wanted to learn or do or become. I named this the *Confirming Mentoring Style* [Style 4]. It is denoted by "**mP**" in my Model because the protege is more dominant during interactions with the mentor. This Style is especially appropriate when the protege is *Consciously Competent* (*aware & able*) – has ideas, decisions or actions to propose, or feelings and concerns to express.

After identifying those mentoring behaviors that defined each of the four

Mentoring Styles, I realized that the Informational and Guiding Styles **equipped** the protege with what the mentor knows, whereas the Collaborative and Confirming Styles **empowered** what the protege wants to learn, do and become.

It's important to emphasize that these Mentoring Styles are not something a mentor *does to* a protege, but are actually *different styles of relating* at any moment in time. Effective mentors *provide* these different Styles and successful proteges are *receptive* and *utilize* them, by engaging in corresponding behaviors.

For example, the protege needs to receive and act on the mentor's wise counsel, suggestions, feedback, etc. – for *equipping* to occur.

The protege must take risks, propose decisions and actions, and enter into dialogue – for *empowering* to occur.

### *Reuse any Mentoring Style & behavior when appropriate*

Never think of these 4 Mentoring Styles as 'stages' (1,2,3,4) you progress through only once – even though I label these 4 Mentoring Styles like this:

> ➤ Style 1 [S1] is the Informational Mentoring Style.

> ➤ Style 2 [S2] is the Guiding Mentoring Style.

> ➤ Style 3 [S3] is the Collaborative Mentoring Style.

> ➤ Style 4 [S4] is the Confirming Mentoring Style.

To underscore what I just emphasized, I'm going to explain the 4 Mentoring Styles in this sequence – S4, S3, S2, S1 – because today's  proteges often prefer to be *empowered* by Styles 4&3 so they can learn, do and become what they desire – more than being *equipped* by Styles 2&1 ("told what to do").

Chapter 4 has a Transcript of how I *empowered* my protege (Elaine) to "tell me" what she wanted to do and how she proposed to do this – until she realized that she needed *equipping* from me to succeed.

## 4 Mentoring Styles
## & Associated Mentoring Behaviors

Style 4: The **Confirming Mentoring Style** (=mP in the Model) *empowers* the protege (**P**) to take more initiative and responsibility to handle situations – especially when the protege is functioning at a *Consciously Competent Level* (aware & able). The mentor (**m**) employs the following behaviors:

○ **m is Sounding Board** for protege's contributions, ideas and plans (listens & acknowledges what protege communicates).

○ **m Paraphrases** (listens & reflects back) protege's ideas and feelings.

○ **m Summarizes** (listens & summarizes back) key points protege communicates, to identify them.

- o **m Clarifies** protege's ideas, decisions, and action plans when these seem unrealistic or vague.

- o **m Encourages** protege's internal motivation and ideas that are likely to succeed.

- o **m Blesses P's Dream** or long-term goal/passion to motivate protege into action.

Style 3: The **Collaborative Mentoring Style** (=MP in the Model) is appropriate for *empowering* a Protege (**P**) who is *Consciously Competent* – has enough experience and ability to work *collaboratively* with a Mentor (M). **M&P** employ these behaviors, with no one dominating:

- o **Two-way Dialogue** jointly contributes ideas and solutions to problems.

- o **Jointly Make Decisions** about ideas and actions.

- o **Jointly Solve Problems** by proposing ideas and solutions.

- o **Jointly Plan** tasks or action steps they agree to carry out.

Style 2: The **Guiding Mentoring Style** (=Mp in the Model) is appropriate for a protege (**p**) who is functioning at the *Consciously Incompetent* Level (aware, but unable). This protege has some experience and ability to handle a particular situation, but needs to be *equipped* with different kinds of Mentor (M) *guidance* to be successful:

- o **M Suggests** what protege might do (options to consider implementing, but not imposed in any way).

- o **M Persuades** protege to employ a particular suggestion, or think in a new way.

- o **M Confronts** what protege does or says so protege makes a decision to act (or not act) – without making protege defensive.

- o **M Coaches** protege to learn new skills (demonstrates or models these behaviors).

- o **M Asks Leading Questions** to guide protege's thinking in a certain direction or to influence a new perspective.

- o **M Probes** (via comments / questions) to get protege to think more deeply, instead of simply reacting emotionally to a situation.

Style 1: The **Informational Mentoring Style** (=M in the Model) is appropriate when an inexperienced protege lacks awareness & expertise (at the *Unconsciously Incompetent* Level) and thus needs to be *equipped* with different kinds of information and direction to handle an unfamiliar or highly crucial situation where mistakes must not be made. Always "**ask permission**" before employing any of these Informational Style behaviors (so the protege will be receptive and will utilize what is provided):

o **M Self-Discloses** how he/she handled or mishandled a situation similar to the protege's, to impart "lessons learned."

o **M Describes** how the protege's colleagues handled or mishandled a similar situation, to impart subtle lessons about what works or doesn't work.

o **M Teaches** important concepts and principles so protege understands what to do and why.

o **M Explains** important do's and don'ts, procedures, policies, customs, unwritten rules.

o **M Arranges for Secondary Mentoring** to be provided for brief periods by someone who has experience/expertise the mentor lacks.

o **M Praises** protege's behaviors to provide positive feedback and to motivate these behaviors recurring. [Do not praise the protege personally.]

o **M Advises** what to do (provides *wise counsel* that is not the same as *clinical counseling* for deep-seated problems).

o **M Prescribes** exactly what the protege should do to avoid mistakes (a step-by-step procedure or "game plan" to follow, in an especially critical situation).

**MENTORS:**
When you employ appropriate Mentoring Styles/behaviors, you *equip* and *empower* proteges to progress to higher ***Levels of Awareness and Competence***, so the protege can resolve a challenging situation. This so important I'm repeating this below:

o **Unconsciously Incompetent** (Level 1) – *unaware* of what to do in a particular situation and *unable* (lacks needed competence to do anything).

o **Consciously Incompetent** (Level 2) – *aware* of what to do, but still *unable* (lacks needed competence).

o **Consciously Competent** (Level 3) – *aware* of what to do and *able* to function successfully.

In Chapter 4, I describe how I *equipped* and *empowered* my protege to progress from "clueless" (Level 1) to make a career *transition* and needed inner *transformation* at Level 3.

**PROTEGES:**
You can request appropriate Mentoring Styles/behaviors to **manage your mentor** to provide the *equipping* and *empowering* you need to achieve your goals. You can progress through an inner transformational process needed to make an important external transition in your career or life.

In Chapter 7, I describe how I ***managed my mentor*** to help me:

✓ Make the *transition* from salaried Professor to Business owner, who generates his own income.

✓ Make required *transformations* in my thinking, motivation and actions.

**Summarized Tips for Mentors:**
1. A full competency requires: *understanding, right attitude*, and *behavioral skills, awareness*. Make sure you have all four components to employ Mentoring Style Flexibility as a competency.
2. "***Ask permission***" before providing the *Informational* Mentoring Style so the protege will be receptive, instead of rejecting "being told what to do."
3. Remember: Do not "get stuck" employing your *most* preferred Mentoring Style(s) and associated behaviors. Learn to use your *least* preferred Style(s).

**Summarized Tips for Proteges:**
1. Ask your mentor to provide different kinds of assistance (Mentoring Style Flexibility) – instead of "getting stuck" overly employing a preferred Mentoring Style or behavior.
2. Remember: Do not "get stuck" wanting only your most preferred Mentoring Style and associated behaviors to be provided.
3. If you tend to resist certain kinds of mentor assistance, ask your mentor to "*ask permission*" before employing these behaviors so you will be receptive.

**Summarized Tips for Coordinators & Champions:**
1. Hire an acknowledged *Expert in Partner Training* (as described throughout this book). This Expert should:
   o Enable "strangers" to "become partners" by doing partner activities together.
   o Explain: (a) the negative consequences that result from "getting stuck" on a Preferred Mentoring Style and associated behaviors, and (b) the positive consequences of a "dynamic" interaction.
   o Train partners to engage in *Situational Mentoring* (Mentoring Style Flexibility).
   o Facilitate activities so partners gain the *same* understanding, develop positive attitudes, and employ behavioral skills – so that mentoring actually takes place.
2. Order my ***Mentoring for Results Workbook*** and training materials to *Enhance Mentoring Relationships and Benefits*.
3. Do NOT simply give an **ORIENTATION** or **PEP TALK** – this does NOT **train** mentoring skills needed to function successfully as partners.
4. Do NOT train only mentors or only proteges – because mentoring partners will NOT know what to do when they get together.

#####

# Chapter 3

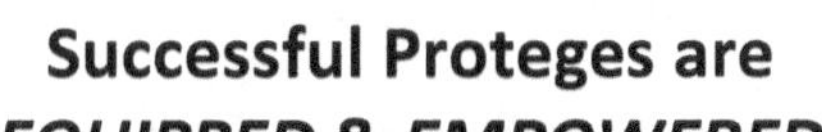

## Successful Proteges are
## *EQUIPPED & EMPOWERED*

Chapter 1 described *Mentoring Styles* **and
behaviors** that *equip* and *empower* proteges.

**Chapter 3 describes:**

- ➢ Negative consequences that result when proteges "get stuck" wanting only *equipping* or only *empowering*.

- ➢ 6 reasons for *equipping* proteges with what mentors know, plus actual examples of benefits.

- ➢ 6 reasons for *empowering* proteges, plus actual examples of benefits.


### How Proteges Can "Get Stuck"
### Wanting To Be *Equipped*

My research revealed that some proteges "got stuck" **wanting to be equipped** with what mentors knew. They were often new to a situation and wanted information and guidance to avoid making needless mistakes. So, they constantly asked mentors for advice and direction ("picked the mentor's brain") instead of showing initiative or problem-solving on their own.

At first, mentors were quite flattered to share their experience and expertise. But when proteges persisted in this behavior, mentors began to view them as too *dependent*.

In order to force these proteges to be more *independent*, mentors stopped meeting with them. Eventually, these relationships died.

In sum, we found that persistently providing too much equipping, or seeking it too much, caused the mentor-protege *relationship* to deteriorate. This consequently resulted in protege goals not being met.

## How Proteges Can "Get Stuck"
## Wanting To Be *Empowered*

Some proteges "got stuck" **wanting to be empowered** to implement their ideas because they were overly self-confident and self-reliant. They tended to be highly motivated self-starters and creative problem-solvers, who could readily propose innovative ideas and usually discover what to do.

Busy mentors eagerly anticipated working with them, because the relationship wouldn't take up much time and they thought they would learn from these proteges. The relationship ran smoothly, until proteges were on the verge of doing something disastrous, but rejected the greater wisdom of their mentors.

Upon realizing that these proteges would not listen to their wise counsel, mentors withdrew support. At this point, the relationship fell apart.

This same phenomenon was later documented in the well-known book, ***Breaking the Glass Ceiling: Can Women Reach the Top of America's Largest Corporations?*** This 1987 book reported that 100% of the females who reached top corporate levels, listened to their *informal* mentor's wise counsel and utilized this successfully. In contrast, 38% of the females being *informally* mentored did not heed their mentor's wise counsel, so these high-level male mentors withdrew assistance, and their protege's career advancement derailed.

This doesn't occur in a well-planned *formalized* mentoring program.

In sum, I have repeatedly found that mentor-protege relationships deteriorate when mentors persistently *empower* proteges to figure out what to do when they cannot do this, or when proteges overly seek out *empowering* for their ideas even though they do not know what to do to be successful.

Bottom line: "Getting stuck" as a mentor or protege results in relationships ending and protege goals not being met.

Now, I want to share what I've discovered about the importance of *both equipping and empowering proteges*, and describe 12 examples reported by my clients.

## The Importance of *Equipping* Proteges

Throughout nearly all of human history, the mentor's main function was to *equip* less-experienced proteges with what the mentor knew. This had to be done because there were no books available on a mass scale, no public education, and no formal training in the workplace. The only way for a novice to "learn the ropes" on a sailing ship, or learn the "tricks of the trade" needed to be a craftsman or merchant, or learn any occupation, was to be attached to more experienced persons, who mentored them.

This attachment occurred *formally*, within the guild and patronage systems, and usually lasted for 4-7 years until a prescribed level of mastery was attained.

Back then, proteges were essentially *empty vessels* into which mentors poured their wisdom, practical know-how and expertise. From this classical concept of mentoring came our dictionary definition: a mentor is a person who provides wise counsel, a trusted guide, an advisor, and a confidant. In these ways, mentors *equipped* proteges to develop themselves in order to earn a livelihood.

When books and public education became more commonplace, such *formalized* mentoring was not needed as much. And so, mentoring went behind the scenes and was provided *informally* – for a chosen few proteges. Much like a puppeteer or Mafia godfather, these mentors pulled strings or made things happen to highlight their protege's talents and sponsor their career advancement.

Mentors usually chose proteges similar to themselves and *equipped* them with their greater experience and wisdom. More often than not, the mentors were males and so were the proteges they chose to help.

This "old boy's network" typically excluded women and minorities. The consequence of this *informal* mentoring was to maintain the status quo more than to initiate innovation or change.

As a counter measure, *formalized* mentoring programs began to be created and proliferate in the late 1970s. They were primarily started to assist women and minorities (as proteges), but also included white males to avoid a new kind of discrimination. The focus was mostly on *equipping* proteges with what mentors know, to shorten the learning curve or increase competency and performance.

This concept of *mentor as equipper* is still prevalent in many mentoring programs – and for six very important reasons (i.e., benefits to be produced):

1.  Equipping proteges imparts practical know-how and wisdom.
2.  Equipping proteges ensures they apply what they learn (this prevents the *transfer-of-training problem*).
3.  Equipping proteges orients them to the organization.
4.  Equipping proteges disseminates and retains intellectual capital.
5.  Equipping proteges enhances their person-job fit.
6.  Equipping proteges reduces costly employee turnover.

Let's examine each reason for *equipping* proteges with what mentors know. This can be done only by a person who has "been there and done that" and thus is functioning at a ***Consciously Competent Level*** – is *aware* of all the important variables in a particular situation and is *able* to do what's required for success.

[Chapter 4 provides a transcribed scenario in which I helped my protege progress from being *Unconsciously Incompetent* to become *Consciously Competent*. I *empowered* what my protege wanted to do and *equipped* her with what I know, so she could make a personal **transformation** needed for making a career **transition**.]

As you read the six examples of *equipping* below, please keep this in mind:

1. You can also benefit in these same ways.

2. Seldom is only equipping or only empowering provided for challenging situations. I've found that both are needed for protege success. However, I emphasize equipping in the six examples described below because this was primarily needed to satisfy the main reason for starting a particular *formalized* mentoring program. In the next chapter, I emphasize empowering because this was primarily needed to satisfy the main reason for starting those programs.

3. Nearly every *formalized* mentoring program I've developed was started for multiple reasons – to produce benefits for proteges, their mentors, and their organization.

4. As mentioned previously, over 80% of the 150 *formalized* mentoring programs I've helped to develop were started to support Equal Employment Opportunity or Affirmative Action or Diversity Initiatives. So, assume that one of these reasons was also involved in all 12 examples you'll read.

**Six Examples of Benefits
from *Equipping* Proteges**

**1. Equipping proteges imparts practical know-how and wisdom:**

Books and training courses cannot do this as well as mentors can, because mentors impart "lessons learned" from real world experience. This occurred at **Ernst & Young**, where our web-based Mentoring Management System® was used to match female proteges to mentors, who *equipped* them with practical know-how and wisdom while helping them develop core competencies needed to become E&Y Partners. This nation-wide *formalized* mentoring program increased E&Y's female Partners by 13% over four years and decreased female turnover that saved $10 million annually.

**2. Equipping proteges prevents the *transfer-of-training* problem:**

Regardless of how well designed or delivered training is, learners typically have a problem applying this correctly and appropriately in varied, real world situations. This *transfer-of-training problem* is so rampant in white-collar professions that a well-known adage describes the irrelevance of getting university degrees:

B.S. stands for Bull Shit;

M.S. is More of the Same;

Ph.D. means Piled Higher and Deeper.

Here is just one example:

At **Scotiabank**, newly hired MBAs from the best universities were found to have little to no practical understanding of current banking practices. So, Scotiabank created training courses to enable them to learn 103 competencies needed to become Commercial Loans Officers.

Internal evaluations indicated that they were really "learning about" these competencies (this took 12 months on average) without developing actual "know-how" to use them in real world situations.

I was asked to develop a *formalized* mentoring program in which these MBAs would (1) take an existing course and then (2) be matched with a mentor (bank manager), who would help them apply with customers what they had learned in class.

This 2-step process connected "knowing about" the competencies with "knowing how" to use them, and reduced overall learning time from 12 to 9 months on average. These idealistic new hires learned the realities of current banking. Costly turnover was reduced enough to pay for this *formalized* mentoring program.

### 3. Equipping proteges orients them to the organization:

There will always be a need to orient new employees to the corporate culture and assimilate them to "feel they belong" in the corporate family. If newcomers have a contact person (mentor or sometimes a "buddy"), they will "get up to speed" much faster and won't make career-limiting mistakes or "fall through the cracks" due to neglect. This benefits the organization by preventing chaos, where everyone literally "does one's own thing" because there is no accepted corporate identity or culture.

Mentors can facilitate all of these things better than typical Orientation Programs or Orientation Manuals – and make new hires feel welcomed into the corporate family.

Here is one of my fondest examples because the company owner (Ken Bailey) is my long-time mentor and friend. This was also my first corporate client.

When Ken's software development company (**Pathfinder**) was just a start-up, I developed a mentoring-and-coaching program that enabled it to grow from 7 to 14 to 24 employees over two years, to become a more established company (**StarGarden**) with a corporate identity and culture.

In college, none of Ken's newly hired software programmers had been taught Cognos (the programming language that Ken's software programmers were using to develop software applications). So, I trained programmers to provide systematic coaching within the company to ensure mastery of Cognos.

These same coaching skills were also employed to teach clients how to use the software application being licensed. This produced such a significant reduction in the number of callbacks that the company saved $40,000 or more per year.

**4. Equipping proteges disseminates and retains intellectual capital:**

*Formalized* mentoring is the best way to pass on, retain, and then utilize the intellectual capital that separates one company from its competition. This is becoming increasingly more essential each year as more Baby Boomers approach retirement age. Once they retire, they will take with them their business acumen, practical know-how, and wisdom for making sound judgments, which took them many years of experience to gain.

**Example:** As a first step to address this, **Sony Electronics** created a Talent Management Program for the next generation of Executives. As a second step, to retain the intellectual capital residing at the top levels (within the CEO, COO, CFO, etc.), I was asked to plan a nation-wide *formalized* mentoring program. The goal was for future Executives to develop core leadership competencies that retained and disseminated **Sony Electronics** intellectual capital.

Ray Hartjen (program coordinator) used our web-based Mentoring Management System to match best-fit mentoring partners on Needs/Expertise statements based on the core competencies. Ray monitored mentoring activity to ensure intellectual capital was passed on so it could be retained.

One wonders why more organizations aren't utilizing these soon-to-be retirees as mentors to equip the next generation with intellectual capital before it is too late.

Better yet, why not hire retirees on a part-time basis to be full-time mentors? They have sufficient time and expertise to devote to this essential activity.


**5. Equipping proteges enhances their person-job fit:**

Taking courses and reading books does not adequately prepare a person to make a successful *transition* into a new job or position, because books and courses cannot facilitate needed *inner transformation* like mentors can.

This occurred at **Turner Construction Company** (America's largest and fastest growing construction company) when TCO tried to develop new project managers through training courses (only). Performance Appraisals indicated there was still much to learn about HOW to work harmoniously with architects, bankers, and politicians during early Partnering Sessions.

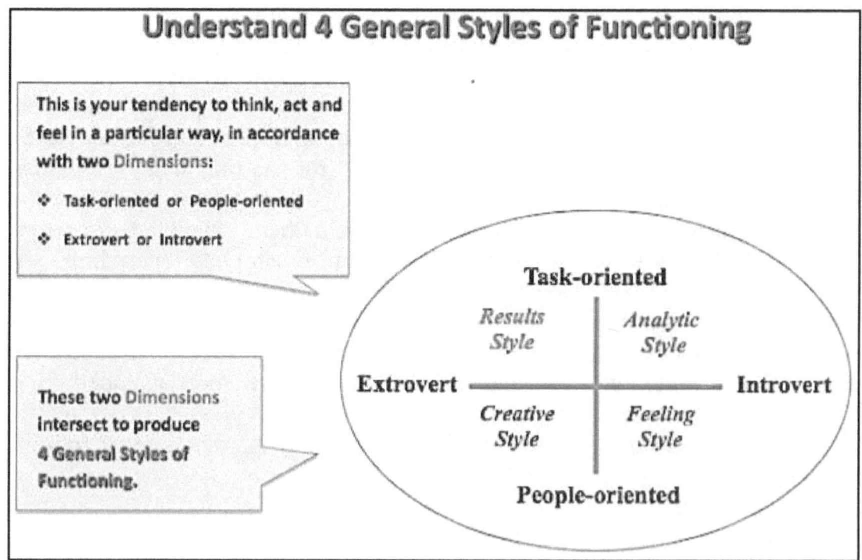


I was asked to facilitate my *Mentoring for Results Partner Training* in four regions across the USA. During training sessions for these four groups, all participants answered my **General Style of Functioning Indicator**. All proteges scored highest on **Results Style**. Their mentors helped these highly **results-oriented** proteges develop a different style of working, thinking, valuing, and communicating so they could work harmoniously with:

> *creative* architects, who frequently changed designs with little concern for added cost and time;

> *analytical* estimators and bankers, who questioned all costs for everything;

> *feeling-oriented* politicians, who wanted to win emotional approval from voters, by addressing their concerns about the environment, disruption to citizens to make space for new construction, and hiring local people (especially the unemployed) for the project.

During training, mentors self-disclosed how they had learned to work harmoniously with these other Styles and how failure to do this stunted career opportunities. Prior to this training, all of these proteges (about 100) valued being only *results-oriented* because they believed "build it on time and on budget" was the key to success.

NOTE: Since 1969, when the well-known book, *The Peter Principle,* was published, we've known that highly capable performers rise to a level where they are incompetent – unless they are *equipped* through mentoring to develop a better person-job fit.

**6. Equipping proteges reduces costly employee turnover:**
Improving the person-job fit and performance prevents poorly performing workers from "leaving the job" physically or psychologically. It costs 1.5 to 2.5 times an employee's salary to recruit, train and replace that person – and costs much more for higher-level leaders and personnel with specialized expertise. So, retaining valued employees is a main reason for starting many *formalized* mentoring programs.

**Jet Propulsion Lab** (JPL) hired me to help them develop a *formalized* mentoring program to reduce costly turnover of "Fresh Outs" (new hires who were *fresh out* of top universities and knew very little about JPL's high performance standards or the cost of living in/near Pasadena or the travel time required for longer commutes). Mentor assistance was so successful in reducing costly "Fresh Out" turnover that all new hires were soon included in an Orientation Mentoring Program.

The money saved from reduced turnover more than paid for two full-time mentoring program coordinators!

I helped them develop different formalized mentoring programs – for *career exploration* to choice the best career path; for *career development* to develop needed technical competencies; for *new leaders* – throughout JPL's Technical Division.

Above, I discussed six reasons I've discovered for *equipping* proteges with what mentors know from greater experience. These reasons correspond to why American companies start mentoring programs, according to Modis Professional Services:

- 73% are started to reduce costly employee turnover
- 71% to improve leadership competencies
- 66% to develop new managers and leaders
- 49% to put high potentials on the fast track
- 48% to support diversity initiatives
- 30% to improve the technical knowledge of staff

In *formalized* mentoring programs that I help organizations develop, I train mentoring partners together so that BOTH *equipping* and *empowering* occurs.

Below, I discuss the importance of ***empowering* proteges** and then highlight this with six examples.

## The Importance of *Empowering* Proteges

Today's better-educated proteges need to be *empowered* by mentors to use their innate intelligence and creative ideas to solve challenging problems, to use their diversity and initiative to pursue desired goals and passionate dreams, and to make innovative contributions so their organization does not stagnate but surpasses competitors.

Did you know that Sir Isaac Newton (1642-1727) was *empowered* to do such things by his mentor, and that this significantly influenced the Industrial Revolution in Great Britain and made it a supreme power at that time?

Sir Isaac Barrow, the only professor of mathematics at Cambridge University (in the 1600-1700s, departments had only one professor), stepped down and gave Newton his singular position because he recognized Newton's innate genius. This empowered the 25-year old Newton to further his work and discoveries on: (a) the Laws of Motion and Universal Gravitation and (b) the differential calculus for solving complex mathematical problems.

Newton disseminated these discoveries by writing the *Principia*, which described the principles of mathematics and mechanics that greatly influenced the Industrial Revolution.

Another mentor, Johannes Kepler, *empowered* its publication by funding this himself. This book is arguably one of the most influential books in the development of Western Civilization.

Do you know that America's unique form of federal government primarily resulted from *mentors empowering* three proteges?

George Wythe mentored Thomas Jefferson while he was a law student at William and Mary College – *empowering* him to learn about and embrace the "democratic ideals" that Jefferson later wrote into the *Declaration of Independence* (this helped launch the American Revolution against England, to create the United States of America, which Jefferson called the "great experiment").

After serving as the third President, Jefferson mentored the fourth President, James Madison – *empowering* him to be the principal author of the *US Constitution* (for which he became known as the "Father of the Constitution").

Jefferson also mentored the fifth President – James Monroe – *empowering* him to create the *Monroe Doctrine*, which stated that America would not tolerate European intervention in the Americas. More importantly, this Doctrine kept the young USA out of Europe's many wars, so its resources could be used for domestic purposes.

Below are six very important ***reasons for empowering proteges.*** You can also benefit in these ways:

1.  Apply what's been taught.
2.  Maintain uniqueness/diversity while fitting in.
3.  Make creative contributions that prevent stagnation of the organization.
4.  Explore career paths to choose the best one.
5.  Change career direction.
6.  Make what's learned more personally meaningful.

## Six Examples of Benefits
## from *Empowering* Proteges

**1. Empowering proteges to apply what's been taught:**
Books, courses, and training enable learners to "know about" concepts and topics, but cannot as readily enable learners to develop the "know-how" associated with usable competencies. Mentors can *empower* proteges to adapt and apply what's been taught so they do develop actual competencies for real world use.

This occurred within the **Air National Guard** (ANG) after I helped them create a *formalized* mentoring program that developed leadership competencies at three career levels:

1. Personal leadership competencies at the Tactical Level (e.g., exercise sound judgment; assess self);

2. Competencies for leading people or teams at the Operational Level (e.g., influence through win/win solutions; promote collaboration and teamwork);

3. Competencies for leading the institution at the Strategic Level (e.g., embrace change and transformation; drive execution).

We installed ANG's leadership competencies into the *Needs/Expertise Inventory* of our web-based **Mentoring Management System** so the program coordinator could use this to quickly and precisely match best-fit mentoring partners and monitor their activity as they carried out online Mentoring Action Plans to develop the competencies.

I also modified my *Mentoring for Results Partner Training* to meet ANG's special requirements, so 110,000 members of the Guard could participate and benefit. ANG wanted participants to be successful in this important Mission-Driven Mentoring Program to fulfill its Mission: To protect the U.S. Constitution, its Government and its People.

**2. Empowering protege's uniqueness/diversity:**
*Empowering* uniqueness and diversity can lead to new business opportunities that also require "fitting in" with established practices. I helped the **Union Bank of California** develop a *formalized* mentoring program for African-American business owners (a) to motivate them to borrow money from Union Bank, (b) to equip and empower them to start and run profitable businesses, and (c) to ensure that the bank loan would be properly used to run and grow the business, (d) so more money would be borrowed, and (e) paid back.

Doing these things enabled Union Bank to achieve its goal of becoming the "Bank of Choice" for African-American business owners.

**3. Empowering proteges to make creative contributions that prevent**

**stagnation of the organization:**

Do you know which company – Fuji Films or Eastman Kodak  – sponsored the 1984 Olympics held in Los Angeles? When Fuji Films won sponsorship, **Eastman Kodak**'s top leaders realized that stagnation had set in and needed to be addressed. So, they focused the Imaging Science Division on creating new hybrid products such as the laser printer, digital camera and photocopier.

This required the integration of expertise in chemistry and electronics – which did not happen as expected. When Kodak realized there were new product delays, they asked me to develop a formalized mentoring program in which *reciprocal mentoring* facilitated:

- ✓ knowledge exchange between researchers with backgrounds in chemistry and electronics to promote understanding of each other's discipline, and

- ✓ empowered the creative contributions each could make to develop innovative hybrid products.

Instead of mandating such creativity and innovative products from the top, better results occur when leaders *empower* this:

- ✓ *Empowering* motivated people at **IBM** produced the first PC, after several years of mandating this from the Top.

- ✓ *Empowering* a team that wanted to create a universal laser printer (to work with any PC) made **Hewlett-Packard** the first world leader in laser jet printers.

- ✓ *Empowering* **3M** employees to innovate new products year after year.

**4. Empowering proteges to explore career paths to choose the best one:**

Choosing the wrong career path hurts both the individual and the organization, especially in high tech companies where many technical personnel choose the *managerial path* because they believe it provides more "perks" (bigger office, parking space, higher salary) than they will get by staying on the *technical path*.

Mentors can *empower* proteges to explore different career options so they gain a realistic understanding of the one that's best for them and the organization, and discover which competencies they need to develop for success.

This occurred within the Hosiery Division of **Sara Lee Corporation**. A survey conducted by its Women's Information Network (WIN) identified two major concerns of female employees: not knowing career development options and lack of mentoring.

So, we collaboratively planned a *formalized* mentoring program in which carefully-matched mentors helped proteges explore interesting career paths, identify one to pursue, and then begin developing requisite competencies.

Formal evaluation revealed that over 85 percent of participants said (a) the program met or exceeded expectations, (b) mentoring partners were well matched, and (c) my *Mentoring for Results® Partner Training* had adequately prepared them to work well together.

## 5. Empowering proteges for new career directions:

Sometimes, proteges want to "take the road not taken" and pursue once-undreamed-of opportunities, such as: earning a degree, relocating to an unfamiliar place, moving laterally into a new part of the organization. This might entail overcoming long-held attitudes, such as overcoming management-labor animosity.

This occurred within **CSX Transportation** when mentors from Management empowered proteges from Labor to take courses and qualify themselves to move into management positions.

Changing career direction is also required when an organization undergoes a major paradigm shift. This occurred at **NCR** when their sales personnel suddenly had to stop selling their own technical *products* (manufacturing became outsourced) and begin selling creative technical *solutions*.

Because the mentoring program I developed for NCR's technical leaders had been successful for several years, I was asked to develop a mentoring program that would *equip* and *empower* "product sellers" to become "creative solution sellers." NCR is still selling creative solutions because of this program.

## 6. Empowering personally meaningful learning:

This occurred at **Varian Associates**, in its Radiation Division. After designing a *formalized* mentoring program to reduce the turnover of High Potentials, we *empowered* them to nominate a mentor who could equip and empower them to engage in personally meaningful learning.

One High Potential had been a member of several project teams, where he was slowly "learning by osmosis" what project managers do. He realized that it could take a long time to learn enough to become a good project manager, and he wanted to do this faster. So, he chose a Senior Vice-President (who had been a top project manager) to be his mentor. After *equipping* this protege with relevant knowledge and skills, the mentor *empowered* the protege to take the lead on working with key people in the Training Department to create a series of Project Management Courses.

**Bottom Line Return on Investment**: Equipping and empowering this *one* protege had a corporate-wide **Transformational Impact**:

- ✓ The protege learned how to function as an excellent project manager, whose projects were completed on schedule and on budget (this made money);
- ✓ This High Potential did not leave the company (this saved replacement costs);
- ✓ The Radiation Division had no prior training course for becoming a project manager (the new courses trained better project managers);
- ✓ The newly empowered/created courses enabled the Radiation Division to move from last place amongst 23 Divisions worldwide – at #23, it was a money loser – to become a profit center.

**Summarized Tips for Mentors:**
1. If your protege seems to "get stuck" only wanting equipping or empowering, "***ask permission***" to discuss this so a "dynamic' relationship develops.
2. Read the importance and examples of *equipping* proteges Then, with your partner, decide which one(s) to pursue.
3. Read the importance and examples of *empowering* proteges Then, with your partner, decide which one(s) to pursue.
4. Identify a protege whom you can equip and empower to produce a *transformational impact* on that protege and on his/her organization.

**Summarized Tips for Proteges:**
1. If your mentor seems to "get stuck" only wanting to provide equipping or empowering, "ask permission" to discuss this so a "dynamic" relationship develops.
2. To prevent failed relationships, do not "get stuck" overly wanting equipping or empowering.
3. Develop a "dynamic relationship" that has both equipping and empowering.
4. As you read the importance and examples of *equipping* proteges, think of a mentor who could assist you in one or more of these ways.
5. As you read the importance and examples of *empowering* proteges, think of a mentor who could assist you in one or more of these ways.
6. Identify a mentor who can *equip* and *empower* you to make a specific *transformational impact* for everyone involved.

**Summarized Tips for Coordinators and Champions:**
1. To prevent failed relationships, ensure partners do not "get stuck" on equipping or empowering.
2. Decide which reasons for *equipping* and *empowering* proteges you will promote in your *formalized* mentoring program.
3. Match mentor-protege partners to promote *transformational impacts* on the protege, mentor and organization. This will more than pay for ALL costs associated with planning and implementing a *formalized* mentoring program.
4. Have an **Expert** provide Partner Training – using proven mentoring activities and materials – that develop *Mentoring Style Flexibility* so *Situational Mentoring* occurs.

#####

# Chapter 4

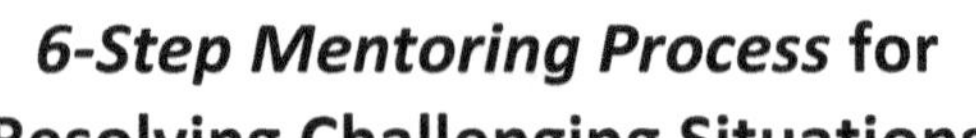

## *6-Step Mentoring Process* for
## Resolving Challenging Situations

**In Chapter 4, you'll learn:**

➢ When to use the 6-Step Mentoring Process & Mentoring Style Flexibility (*Situational Mentoring*).

➢ How Gray's *6-Step Mentoring Process* Provides Effective & Efficient Mentoring – and when this should be done.

➢ How I first empowered and then equipped my protege (Elaine) to progress from the *Unconsciously Incompetent* Level to the *Consciously Incompetent* Level to the *Consciously Competent* Level of ***Awareness & Competence***. [Read ***TRANSCRIPT*** of actual mentoring.]

➢ How everything I did helped Elaine make a *career transition* that required a *personal transformation* in her thinking and actions.

---

You can access an online course that covers what's described in this chapter:
*Mentor One Another – Advanced Training* – to handle difficult challenges
**View PROMO**:   https://graysacademy.teachable.com/p/mentor-one-another-advanced-training

---

### When to use the *6-Step Mentoring Process*
### & *Situational Mentoring*

Because "lack of time" is a common problem, especially for busy mentors, I wanted to discover an *effective* and *time-efficient* method for assisting proteges to handle challenging situations successfully.

I developed a **6-Step Mentoring Process** for *effectively* and *efficiently* assisting proteges to resolve challenging situations, such as these:

o **Transitioning** to a different career or position (the real-life scenarios below and in Chapter 7 illustrate this).

o Making a personal **transformation** in thinking, motivation and actions.

o Deciding what to do when facing a **dilemma**.

o Solving a **complex problem**.

Using this *6-Step Mentoring Process* (a) keeps partners focused on their reason for meeting, so tangential matters do not sidetrack either person, and (b) enables partners to agree on activities and tasks, and (c) put this into a *Mentoring Action Plan* (MAP) that (d) will resolve the challenging situation being discussed.

The MAP provides direction – like a Road MAP – to achieve the agreed upon goal, by converting "talk" into "actions" that produce "results," and enables both partners to come to meetings prepared to do each activity.

Completed MAPs document what was done and achieved – as evidence of *Return on Investment* (ROI). *Informal* mentoring lacks this aspect of *formalized* mentoring.

### I Must Emphasize this Again

While using the 6-Step Mentoring Process, efficient/effective mentors employ **Mentoring Style Flexibility** – that is, they employ any of the four Mentoring Styles and associated behaviors when these are needed to handle the situation. This prevents two common mentor mistakes that I want to point out again:

o Many mentors "tell" proteges what to do, for various reasons: they know what to do because of greater experience; they don't want their partner to make a critical mistake; they believe "giving advice" or "sharing wisdom" is their main role; they lack time to do anything else.

o Many mentors "expect" proteges to figure out what to do, for various reasons: they believe it is the protege's responsibility to do this; they want their protege to "stretch" beyond their comfort zone; they believe the protege has the capability; they don't want to be held responsible for what happens.

You want to avoid both of these mentor mistakes, because they can undermine the mentoring relationship in these ways:

o When mentors "tell" proteges what to do and this doesn't work, this is usually perceived as being the mentor's fault. This can undermine the protege's confidence in, or respect for, the mentor.

o When mentors "expect" proteges to figure out what to do and they cannot, this is usually perceived as being the protege's fault. This can undermine the mentor's confidence in, or respect for, the protege's capability.

## How Gray's *6-Step Mentoring Process* Provides Effective & Efficient Mentoring

Side 2 of my *Mentoring Pocket Card* overviews what I'm going to describe.

---

### 6-Step Mentoring Process™
### for Complex, Challenging Situations

**Step 1. Understand Protege's Needs, Goals, Attitudes, Perceptions**

| | | |
|---|---|---|
| S4 Sounding Board | S4 Clarify P's ideas/feelings | S4 Be non-threatening |
| S4 Summarize ideas | S4 Paraphrase ideas/feelings | S4 Encourage open talking |

**Step 2. Review Protege's Actions & their Consequences**

| | |
|---|---|
| S4 Clarify P's actions & their consequences | S4 Paraphrase P's comments |
| S4 Summarize action-consequence patterns | S2 Probe for deeper realizations |

**Step 3. Identify the Real Issue**

| | |
|---|---|
| S4 Clarify P's real issue M has heard | S1 Self-disclose how M identified a similar real issue |
| S2 Probe to motivate insights | S2 Suggest the real issue M heard P express |
| S1 Explain realities P must accept | S2 Confront incongruent perceptions, attitudes, goals |

**Step 4. Define/Redefine Protege's Goals, Attitudes & Perceptions**

| | |
|---|---|
| S2 Ask Leading Questions to extract ideas | S1 Self-disclose how M made positive changes |
| S2 Persuade to be more positive | S1 Describe how P's peers made changes |
| S4 Paraphrase or Summarize or Encourage anything positive P has said | |

**Step 5. Expand Protege's Thinking to Consider New Options**

| | |
|---|---|
| S1 Self-disclose M's insights/actions | S4 Clarify ideas P mentions or has mentioned |
| S1 Teach pertinent concepts | S1 Arrange for secondary mentoring to be provided |
| S2 Suggest optional actions | S2 Ask Leading Questions to guide creative thinking |

**Step 6. Agree on & Commit to a Workable Action Plan**

| | |
|---|---|
| S3 Two-way dialog of ideas | S3 Alternate Leadership of different steps or tasks |
| S3 Make joint decisions | S1 Give Advice on a logical sequence for action steps |
| S3 Jointly solve problems | S4 Clarify P's commitment to carry all action steps |
| S2 Suggest left-out, key steps | S2 Confront what P might do to sabotage action plan |

*© 1990-2005 Corporate Mentoring Solutions Inc.*

---

This **6-Step Mentoring Process** guides mentor-protege interactions, gives this a natural flow, and keeps it focused on the main reason for meeting – so neither the mentor or protege wastes time getting sidetracked on tangential matters.

Beneath each Step I've listed the Mentoring Styles (S1, S2, S3, S4) and associated behaviors I most often use:

> S1 for the Informational Mentoring Style

> S2 for the Guiding Mentoring Style

> S3 for the Collaborative Mentoring Style

> S4 for the Confirming Mentoring Style

NOTE: S1, S2, S3, and S4 do not connote "Stages" or "Steps" – but are merely used here to indicate the four Mentoring Styles.

Previously, I emphasized that Mentoring Styles can be used in any order, over and over as needed, because they are not "Stages."

**Step 1. Understand Protege's Needs, Goals, Attitudes and Perceptions**

Mentors should use the Confirming Style behaviors below to initiate interaction with a protege during Step 1 – because this empowers the protege to talk openly and honestly about an especially challenging situation.

This reveals the protege's goals, attitudes and perceptions [GAPs]. These are often negative or unproductive at this point, and are thus not appropriate for handling the situation.

Proteges will likely be functioning at the **Unconsciously Incompetent** Level -- *unaware* of what to do and *lacking competence* needed to handle the situation they describe. [lower case "**m**" indicates mentor plays a supportive role; capital "**P**" indicates protege plays an active role]

o S4 **m** is **Sounding Board** (just listen)

o S4 **m Clarifies** P's ideas/feelings

o S4 **m** is **Non-threatening, non-judgmental**

o S4 **m** is **Encouraging**

o S4 **m Summarizes** key ideas P proposes

o S4 **m Paraphrases** ideas/feelings P expresses

o S2 **M Asks Probing and Leading Questions** to guide discussion

**Step 2. Protege Realizes Actions and Consequences**

By using the behaviors below, mentors can help proteges realize what they have done about their situation – and whether this has produced desired positive consequences, or not.

Typically, protege actions have not worked – that is why the protege is talking with the mentor. Listen carefully for those actions that have produced both negative and positive consequences.

o S4 **m Clarifies** Protege's actions and their consequences

o S4 **m Summarizes** action-consequence patterns P describes

- o S2 **M Probes** for deeper realizations
- o S4 **m Paraphrases** P's comments

## Step 3. Identify the Protege's Real Issue

What a protege initially presents during Steps 1 and 2 is usually just the "presenting issue" – not the "real issue" causing the difficult situation or preventing its resolution.

To avoid wasting valuable time and effort on the wrong issue, use these mentoring behaviors to identify the "real issue":

- o S4 **m Clarifies** P's real issue that M heard
- o S1 **M Self-discloses** how he/she resolved a similar issue (or failed to do so)
- o S2 **M Probes** to motivate new insights or deeper thinking
- o S2 **M Suggests** possible "real issues" the protege expressed
- o S1 **M Explains** realities protege must accept
- o S2 **M Confronts** incongruent perceptions, attitudes, goals expressed by protege, indecision

## Step 4. Develop Productive Goals, Attitudes and Perceptions

Unproductive goals, attitudes or perceptions [GAPs] hinder a protege from handling a situation successfully. Helping proteges develop productive goals, attitudes and perceptions enables them to progress from being **Unconscious** to being **Conscious** (more aware of what's important to do).

The mentor's goal is to help the protege progress from (Level 1) being **Unconsciously Incompetent** to (Level 2) being **Consciously Incompetent** to (Level 3) being **Consciously Competent** – is *aware* of what to do in a particular situation and is *able* to do it.

- o S2 **M Asks Leading Questions** to extract ideas
- o S1 **M Self-discloses** how M handled a situation like the protege's
- o S2 **M Persuades** protege to be more positive or take particular action
- o S1 **M Describes** how protege's peers handled or mishandled a similar situation
- o S4 **m Paraphrases** or **Summarizes** or **Encourages** what P says

## Step 5. Expand Protege's Thinking to Consider New Options

Steps 1-4 get the protege ready to consider new options for handling the situation – without being defensive when the mentor employs *equipping* behaviors.

**NOTE:** Mentors should "**ask permission**" before providing Style 1 or 2 mentoring behaviors – because many of today's proteges want to be *empowered*, and might reject *equipping*.

The mentor can now expand the protege's thinking in two key ways: (1)

directly by sharing their own thoughts and actions, or (2) indirectly by arranging for other people to provide assistance (when the mentor lacks relevant experience or expertise).

- o S1 **M Self-discloses** own insights/actions that worked in a similar situation
- o S2 **M Asks Leading Questions** to guide creative thinking
- o S4 **m Clarifies** ideas P mentions
- o S1 **M Teaches** pertinent concepts
- o S1 **M Arranges** help from secondary mentors who are like the protege (gender, etc.)
- o S2 **M Suggests** optional actions for protege to consider implementing

**Step 6. Agree on a *Mentoring Action Plan* to Handle Protege's Situation**

This step converts *Talk* into *Actions* that produce desired *Results*. The Mentoring Action Plan [MAP] provides a ***Road Map*** for what to do to achieve intended Goals, and provides an agreed upon *Schedule for Action Steps*.

By this point in the 6-Step Mentoring Process, the protege will likely be aware of those actions needed to accomplish a productive Goal and thus can *Collaborate* on writing down these action steps.

Sometimes, the mentor might need to use *Informational* or *Guiding* Style behaviors, such as those below. Unless the protege and mentor both agree on the action steps, they both will not commit to carry them out completely to achieve the Goal.

When necessary, revisit any Step that must be resolved satisfactorily in preparation for another Step. Throughout the interaction, the mentor should remain non-threatening and non-judgmental so the protege will talk openly and honestly.

- o S3 **M&P** engage in **Two-way dialogue** of ideas
- o S2 **M Confront** indecision or what protege might do to sabotage action plan
- o S2 **M Suggests** key action steps for protege to consider implementing
- o S3 **M&P Make Joint Decisions**
- o S1 **M Gives Advice** on a logical sequence for action steps
- o S3 **M&P Jointly Solve Problems**
- o S4 **m Clarifies** P's commitment to carry all action steps

**<u>Two important questions:</u>**

- Do all proteges need the *same equipping* provided by Informational and Guiding Mentoring Styles?
- Do all proteges need the *same empowering* provided by Collaborative and Confirming Mentoring Styles?

No, we haven't found this to be the case, as we've trained over 40,000 mentors and proteges at different stages in their careers.

Newer hires with little real world experience and limited competence typically need more equipping (than empowering) from mentors to get up to speed and learn the ropes; they also need some empowering to apply what they're learning.

In contrast, proteges who are future leaders or executives bring much more experience and capability into the mentoring relationship; hence, they usually need a lot more empowering to express and implement their vision for the organization; they also need some equipping to learn core competencies to overcome individual gaps.

Between these two extremes is the largest group of proteges. They are interested in exploring different career paths, and developing their talents and competencies, to choose the best career path for them and for their organization. This usually requires a balance of equipping and empowering.

How does a mentor know what's appropriate to provide? By knowing the protege's *Level of Awareness and Competence* relevant to each situation (described in Chapter 3). And by knowing these Situational Factors:

- ✓ Protege's relevant experience pertinent to the situation
- ✓ Urgency of the situation (must the protege act immediately?)
- ✓ Protege's current awareness of important factors in the situation
- ✓ Criticalness of the situation (are trial-and-error efforts acceptable or not?)
- ✓ Protege's current competence or ability to do what's required for success
- ✓ Protege's attitudes and perceptions (e.g., positive or negative)

To know which Mentoring Style/behavior to use at any point, I watch the protege's **body language cues**. These cues provide useful feedback on whether what I say or do is helpful, or not helpful. For example:

- ➢ Facial expression (positive expression shows enthusiasm)
- ➢ Hands  (clenched hands signify resistance to what's being offered)
- ➢ Eye contact  (none indicates avoidance)
- ➢ Leaning  (toward mentor means engagement in discussion)
- ➢ Arms  (folded indicates defensiveness, resistance)
- ➢ Voice (expresses confidence, fear, worry, enthusiasm, etc.)

### Overview of Mentoring my Protege (Elaine)

You are going to read a *TRANSCRIPT* of an actual mentor-protege interaction – to help you integrate what you've learned thus far. This interaction was videotaped as it actually occurred (no script, no rehearsing), then edited into an 18-minute *Mentoring for Results Training Video* with clear labeling of what I said as the mentor, and the impact of this on my protege (Elaine).

The ***TRANSCRIPT*** describes how to Style-shift to help a protege progress from being **Unconsciously Incompetent** to become **Consciously Competent** – *aware* of what to do and *able* to handle a challenging situation that cannot be handled on one's own. In Elaine's case, she needed mentoring to make a significant career change – from "Print Advertising" where she was very successful into "Video Advertising" where she "doesn't have a clue" how to make a video. This is what she told me and why she asked for my mentoring assistance.

While mentoring Elaine, I followed the **6-Step Mentoring Process**, took account of Situational Factors, and watched for body language cues – as described previously.

Below is a ***Transcription*** of what took place. For each mentor statement (M-1, M-2, etc.), I have indicated the Mentoring Style (S1, S2, S3, S4) and have **bolded the associated mentoring behavior** that I provided for my protege (P):

- o S1 indicates the Informational Mentoring Style followed by an **associated behavior**

- o S2 indicates the Guiding Mentoring Style followed by an **associated behavior**

- o S3 indicates the Collaborative Mentoring Style followed by **an associated behavior**

- o S4 indicates the Confirming Mentoring Style followed by an **associated behavior**

As you read, notice how I used particular Mentoring Style behaviors (and why) to guide my protege through these **Levels of Awareness  and Competence** – from Level 1 to 3 – so she could change careers:

- ➤ **Unconsciously Incompetent** (Level 1) – <u>unaware</u> of what to do in a particular situation and <u>unable</u> (lacks needed competence to do anything).

- ➤ **Consciously Incompetent** (Level 2) – <u>aware</u> of what to do, but still <u>unable</u> (lacks needed competence).

- ➤ **Consciously Competent** (Level 3) – <u>aware</u> of what to do and <u>able</u> to function successfully.

### *TRANSCRIPT* of
### *Mentoring For Results Training Video*
### *(Mentoring Elaine)*

### Step 1: Understand Protege's Needs, Goals, Attitudes and Perceptions

**Protege-1:** You know I've been here at this advertising agency for about 8 years now, and I think I've done a pretty good job in the print areas for many clients. I do all the corporate brochures and all the annual reports for Simpco Toys, and I think they're pretty happy with the work I do. But, I've come up with a new idea that I'd like to do for them. I've always wanted to try this, but I've got no experience making a video. And if I do it and fail, they're not going to be happy with it; I don't even know that they're going to want me to do it. I'm afraid that if I propose the idea to them, they may think it's a great idea and take it to another advertising agency that has experience making videos. I was thinking of approaching my boss about it, but I'm not sure he's even going to let me do it. I'm really afraid that if I do try something like this, I could make a mess of it: I could fail. I could lose my client. My boss won't be impressed with me. This is a really competitive business, and you don't get a second chance. I feel like I'm in a rut – doing the same thing for so long – but don't have a clue what to do. [Elaine is at the *Unconsciously Incompetent Level* – *unaware* of what to do and *unable* to do anything.]

[NOTE: At the beginning of a mentor-protege interaction, the mentor mostly employs the *Confirming* Mentoring Style in order to: (1) **Encourage** the protege to talk. (2) Be **Non-threatening** and **Non-judgmental** so protege will talk openly and honestly. (3) Be a **Sounding Board** so the protege can express ideas, concerns, etc.]

Did you notice how much Elaine told me –
after "bottling this up" for so many years?

**Mentor-1:** Elaine, let me summarize what I've heard you say to be sure I understand it. You've had an idea to move from print advertising into video advertising – to make a video ad. [S4 Listen to **summarize** and **paraphrase** key points]

**P-2:** Yes.

**M-2:** I've also heard you say that you're a bit hesitant because there are several risks involved. It also sounds like you want to get out of your rut and you can't quite figure out how to do it at this point. [S4 Listen to **clarify** attitudes, perceptions, and emotional concerns.]

**P-3:** Yeah. [I notice these body language cues: protege is leaning away from me, both fists tightly clenched indicating tension, voice lacks enthusiasm. I notice this continuing for the next 15-20 minutes.]

**M-3:** So, your Goal, as I hear you express it, is to move from print advertising into video advertising. Is this your Goal? [S4 Listen to **clarify** ideas into realizable, achievable Goal.]

**P-4:** Yeah! [Nods in agreement]

### Step 2: Review Protege's Actions and Consequences

**M-4:** Have you done anything at this point, or is this just an idea in your head? [S2 Ask **probing question** to get protege to recall what's been done.]

**P-5**: I've been thinking about it for quite a long time now, about two years, and it's been driving me crazy, but I haven't done anything or really talked to anybody, except you right now.

**M-5:** So, there aren't any consequences that have come out of any actions at this point. [S2 Ask **probing question** to get protege to think about possible consequences.]

**P-6:** [sighs – indicating realization and agreement; body language cues still the same]

**M-6:** The only consequences are still in your head.

**P-7:** Yeah. I guess so, when you put it that way.

**M-7:** And right now they seem more on the negative side than the positive side. [S4 **Summarize** consequences based on listening to what protege says.]

**P-8:** [Nods in agreement]

**M-8:** What would you like me to help you do at this point? I've been doing some listening. Has this been enough to help you go away and handle this on your own? Or, do you need something else? [S2 Ask **probing question** to find out assistance protege thinks she needs.]

**P-9:** I think I'd like some advice from you.

---

**Question for you:**
Would *you* give advice?
If so, exactly what advice would *you* give?

**M-9:** I'm certainly willing to provide that, but before I give you advice, could we discuss a few other things? [S2 **Ask leading question** to get permission to provide other types of assistance that protege has not requested, so this will be well received.]

### Step 3: Identify the Protege's Real Issue

**M-10:** I've been listening very carefully and I think I've heard you articulate your real issue. Would you like me to tell you what I've heard? [S2 **Ask leading question** to get permission to describe the real issue]

**P-10**: Sure. [Still not very enthusiastic or comfortable]

**M-11:** OK. I think I detect a fear of failure and that's why you don't want to proceed. [S2 **Ask leading question** to lead protege to confirm she has been stalled by her fears.]

**P-11:** Well, I guess I am kind of afraid of failure, but I could lose my job, my boss could be really unhappy with me even if he doesn't fire me. I could lose my client. And I could look really foolish out there trying to do something I don't know how to do. So, I feel it's pretty valid to be afraid. [Protege confirms that she is at the *Unconsciously Competent Level*.]

**M-12:** If we could come up with a way so you could continue to do your job well and continue to get accolades from your clients and your boss, would that help overcome this fear of failure? [S4 **Clarifies** commitment to pursue an additional, related Goal.]

**P-12:** Yeah.

**M-13:** So, if we can do that, would the Goal to move from print to video advertising still be a Goal you'd want to pursue?

**P-13:** Well, yeah. I think I would.

**M-14:** Let's do a "what if" scenario. What if you continue to do exactly what you're doing now, what will be the consequences of that? [S2 Because protege seems hesitant to commit, **ask probing question.** This prompted a different kind of negative consequence – which can be used to confront other negative consequences already expressed.]

**P-14:** Yeah. I'd probably continue to be a little bit bored and feel a little bit stagnating, but.... [Protege is going to play the "Yes, but" game, where she seemingly agrees, then disagrees or objects – so I interject a question to prevent this.]

**M-15:** Do you want that to happen? [S2 To prevent protege form playing the "Yes, but" game, **confront** what protege says, to motivate her to pursue her new Goal.]

**P-15:** No. It's already happening. I guess that's why I'm toying with the idea of making the video. [Protege still seems to be "toying" with pursuing her Goal.]

**M-16:** OK. Can you think of anything else that could happen as a consequence if you keep doing what you're doing now? [S2 **Ask probing question** – again this prompted a negative consequence.]

**P-16:** Well, I do know I could be left behind, because more clients want video advertising. [Another negative consequence that can be used to confront protege's indecision to pursue her Goal]

**M-17:** I hear you saying that there are actually some very good reasons for you to get over this fear of failure and get on with this new Goal. [S4 **Paraphrase** all the negative consequences from doing nothing as good reasons to pursue the Goal.]

**P-17:** Yeah. I guess I've been sitting on the fence for nearly two years and can't really decide to do it or not to do it.

**M-18:** I'm willing to help you make the decision, and then whatever decision you make, help you carry that out. So, what is your decision? [S1 **Explain** what you are willing to do; S2 **Confront** protege's *indecision* (not the protege herself) so she will make a decision.]

**P-18:** [sighs] I think I'm going to have to go for it because, if I don't, I could be out of a job anyway.


**Step 4: Develop More Productive Goals, Attitudes and Perceptions**

**M-19:** Can you see some ways of turning these potential negative consequences into some positives? [S2 **Ask leading question** to draw out protege's ideas.]

**P-19:** [sighs – without answering].

**M-20:** I guess what I'm saying is this: If you approach it like a lot of bad things can happen, they probably will. So, can we start to think in a more positive, more productive way? [S1 **Explain** what might happen; S2 When this doesn't work, **persuade** protege to think more positively.]

**P-20:** OK. I do know one client – Simpco Toys – really well and I know they're happy with my work. So, it's possible that they might be quite positive for me to produce a video for them. There is one guy in their Corporate Communications, who might really help my situation because we get along pretty well.

**M-21:** So, this client could support you in wanting to go in this new direction. [S4 **Paraphrase** protege's idea – to confirm protege's Goal to make a video ad.]

## Step 5: Expand Protege's Thinking to Consider New Options

**M-22:** Do you feel able to go off and start working on your Goal on your own? [S4 **Clarify** protege's awareness of what to do and ability to do it, based on listening to protege thus far.]

**P-22**: I don't even know where to start. It feels overwhelming to me. I've just made a commitment to do it, but I don't know how to do it. I don't have a clue how to get started. [Protege is still functioning at the *Unconsciously Incompetent Level* – *unaware* of what to do and *unable* to do anything.]

**M-23:** What help do you need from me at this point? [S2 **Ask probing question** to find out what protege thinks she wants.]

**P-23:** [does not answer]

**M-24:** Let's look at your Mentoring Style Indicator. Your highest, most Preferred Mentoring Style is Collaboration – exchanging ideas back and forth. We've done a little bit of that. [S4 **Summarize** assistance already provided.]

**P-24:** Yes. We have.

**M-25:** But you're saying that you need something else right now. What Mentoring Style or behaviors do you need from me? [S2 **Ask probing question** to find out what protege thinks she wants.]

**P-25:** Maybe you could give me some advice.

**Question for you:**

Elaine asked for advice again. Would *you* give advice now?

If so, exactly what advice would *you* give?

**M-26:** I could certainly do that. In fact, your second most preferred Mentoring Style is to seek advice.

**P-26:** Yeah ... sounds reasonable in my situation.

**M-27:** To tap into what I know, so you'll know it too. We could certainly do that, but before we do that, I think I'd rather explore some other options. Is this all right with you? [S2 **Ask leading question** to get permission to provide assistance not requested, so protege will be receptive.]

**P-27:** OK. Sure! [I notice all these body language cues for the first time: protege is leaning forward towards me, fist finally unclenched as she relaxes, voice is enthusiastic and positive.]

**M-28:** Could I throw out some suggestions for you to think about? [S2 **Suggestions** cause protege to think about strategies for solving the problem. I did not offer **advice** – or a **prescription** – because this provides "my" solution. By this point, I had "read" Elaine enough to know she would not be receptive to advice or a prescription because she likes to be in control of deciding what to do and responsible for the consequences.]

**P-28:** OK!

**M-29:** One suggestion that comes to mind is perhaps to take on this project with a partner – with somebody else who already has an expertise in making a video ad, so you can use your strength: your knowledge of the customer. [S2 I **suggested** that Elaine work with a partner based on knowing she must do this since she is *Unconsciously Incompetent – unaware* of what to do and *unable* to do what's required – and she now wants to achieve her Goal quickly, after waiting two years to get started.]

**P-29:** I have that kind of writing expertise, so this would be a possibility. Mary Anne knows how to make video ads. She and I have worked well on other projects. So, she possibly could be my partner.

**M-30:** Would you like for me to share how I encountered a similar situation and finally resolved it, after much agony? [S1 Ask permission to **self-disclose** hard lessons learned in a similar situation, so protege will be receptive to this.]

**P-30:** Sure!

**M-31:** I was in charge of a project, which I initiated, and I realized that I needed someone to co-direct the whole project, because there was a skill set that I quite frankly didn't have, and I was trying to develop the skill set as I was overseeing the project. So, I asked my boss to approve a partner to help me. My boss said, "Fine. You two work together on it." From then on it was a breeze because we complemented each other. Now, for me to do that – and this is the important point here – I had to be willing to share the glory and I had to be willing to give up some control. So, it wasn't just "My Project" any more. It was "Our Project." [S1 While **self-disclosing**, I **explained** what I did without directly telling my protege what to do.]

**P-31:** That's a really good point you've just brought up because I know that I do enjoy having the glory all to myself. Yeah, I'd have to give up some control too. Those really are some issues for me that I hadn't looked at. [Notice how **self-disclosing** causes the protege to *identify two key issues* the mentor had to address in order to be successful; self-disclosing is a powerful way to share what the mentor knows with a protege who likes to figure out what to do.]

**M-32:** So, there could be some other issues we have to deal with. [S4 **Paraphrase** what protege said – to see if she agrees.]

**P-32:** Yeah! There are.

**M-33:** How willing are you to share the glory and give up some control? [S2 **Ask leading question** to draw out how protege will deal with these two key issues.]

**P-33:** I think I could definitely do that – especially now that you pointed it out to me. If I'd been in the situation and I had to do it, I would not have been as comfortable with it. But, when I'm prepared and realize that this is what I have to do, I think I can handle this, because in the long run it's going to get me where I want to go. [Protege is now functioning at the ***Consciously Incompetent Level*** – *aware* she needs a partner, because she is *unable* to make the video ad herself.]

### Step 6: Agree on and Commit to Carry Out a Workable Action Plan to achieve the redefined Goal

**M-34:** We've talked about quite a number of things that you could do and I could help you do. Elaine, are you ready to take what we've talked about and convert it into an Action Plan? [S4 I **clarified** protege's readiness to take action to achieve her Goal – after much talking – because talking alone will not achieve her Goal.]

**P-34**: I don't know if I should talk to my boss first, or go to Simpco Toys, or talk to Mary Anne. I don't really know what to do. [Still functioning at the ***Consciously Incompetent Level***.]

**M-35:** Why don't we write down some of the things that we've talked about you doing and me helping you do? And then, we'll sequence these into a logical Action Plan: what you'll do first, second, and so on. [S1 **Teach** how to create an Action Plan.]

**P-35:** OK!

**M-36:** Let's just start writing down whatever comes to mind – anything we've talked about that could be an action step. Would you do that? [S1 **Teach** what to do to start the Action Planning process, so both partners have input into this process. This creates joint commitment to carry out the agreed-upon Action Plan. Proteges cannot create the Plan on their own; when mentors create the Plan and impose it, I've found that proteges do not commit.]

**P-36:** OK! I could talk to Mary Anne about being my partner.

**M-37:** Yes! If the client says, "We want you to do this new project," they could go to your boss with you – or at least in support of what you want to do. [S2 I **suggested** how my protege could get client buy-in to win over her unsupportive boss.]

**P-37:** That's a really good idea. If I said that my client wants me to do it, this would have more weight with him than if I said I want to do it....

**M-38:** ...because your boss is responsive to customer needs. [S1 **Explain** boss's motivation.]

**P-38a:** Yes! So, I'm just going to put this before talking with my boss. [Mentor helps Elaine sequence 4 action steps she will do: (1) ask professionals how to make a video; (2) find out if Mary Anne will be her partner; (3) get client buy-in; (4) win over boss to support her Goal. Mentor adds input in between each step to prepare protege to carry out each step successfully.]

**P-38b:** [after M&P brainstorm and write down other action steps, Elaine role plays how she will talk with her boss to gain his support] I had a meeting with Simpco Toys the other day and it came to me during the meeting that they could really use video advertising. [Elaine spends 10 minutes describing what she wants to do, and then asks me a question.] What do you think?

**M-39:** It sounds pretty good. Would you like me to give you some feedback? [S1 **Ask leading question** to get permission to give candid **feedbac**k, so protege will be receptive.]

**P-39:** Yes!

**M-40:** OK. Would you like a suggestion? [S2 Ask permission again to give feedback in the form of a **suggestion** that will involve Elaine in deciding what to do.]

**P-40:** Yes! Please.

**M-41:** I suggest you emphasize that you have an idea that will bring in more revenue from a good client, and with your knowledge of this client and their product – their toys – you can do this project a lot better than somebody who doesn't know the client. [S2 My **suggestion** emphasizes appealing to the boss's desire to get *results* by implementing the protege's Goal of making a video advertisement.]

**P-41:** Right. My boss likes results.

**M-42:** So, you will be making more money from a good client. [S1 I again **explain** the results for the company, which will appeal to the boss.]

**P-42:** Yeah!

**M-43:** Because that's what you bring to this project. [S4 **Clarify** protege's contribution once again.]

**P-43:** Right! I can see that would appeal to my boss.

**M-44:** What you don't bring is the process for making the video ad. [S4 **Clarify** protege's main shortcoming.]

**P-44:** Right again!

**M-45:** As we discussed earlier, you need to talk with some people in the video advertising field and with Mary Anne, and then describe how you and Mary Anne will make good partners for this project. [S3 more **discussion** takes place, followed by S2 **coaching** on what to say to the boss.]

**P-45:** I'll get some knowledge about the video advertising field and talk with Mary Anne. This will enable me to feel better prepared to talk with my boss.

**M-46:** Would you say you're committed now to move forward? [S2 **Ask**

**leading question** to get a firm commitment.]

**P-46:** Yes! It's time for me to make a change and I think with your support it'll be a lot easier for me to do that.

**M-47:** OK. I'm willing to help you. [S4 **Encourages** protege's commitment.]

**P-47:** When I looked at the big picture, it all seemed so overwhelming to me. But when you broke it down into small steps that I can do, it's a little easier for me to handle. I'll make a commitment to take action. [Protege validates the value of going through the 6-Step Mentoring Process.]

> At this point, we recorded *brainstormed ideas* discussed in previous Steps and sequenced the best Ideas to be implemented, then put them in our Mentoring Action Plan.
>
> See ***Brainstormed Ideas*** and the resulting ***Mentoring Action Plan*** at the end of this transcript. This 2-step process required another 30 minutes, which is too long to describe here.

**M-48:** OK! As we sequence the four action steps you've agreed to do, you'll keep coming back to me and fill me in on what you've done, what you've learned, where you are. Let's also put into the Action Plan what I'll do as additional action steps. [S2 **Explain** what will happen so protege understands the process and feels comfortable.]

**P-48:** What we should do is schedule a date for meeting again, and I'll make a commitment to have talked with the video professionals by that time. Within two weeks. In that way I'm really committed to getting this started.

**M-49:** Yes, I like that! I've enjoyed our brief time here today discussing this and I'm looking forward to working with you on it.

**P-50:** Me too, Bill!

**M-50:** Thanks for coming in, Elaine.

# *Example of how to*
# Brainstorm Ideas for Action Plan

Protege: *Elaine*    Dept.: *Advertising*    Phone: _______

Mentor: *Bill*    Dept.: *Marketing*    Phone: _______

**Directions:**

1. Separate this top sheet of paper from the one beneath it — to see the **Example** on page 4. Then, place these sheets back **the way they were** — so that everything written on page 2 will be "copied" onto page 4.

2. Agree on a **Major Protege Goal** to be accomplished — Protege then writes it in the center box.

3. Take turns proposing any idea, activity or resource that might help the Protege accomplish his/her Goal. Protege writes down (around center box) what each person proposes. Do this in **5 minutes** by following these **Brainstorming Rules:**

   1. Don't criticize or evaluate ideas now.
   2. Propose lots of ideas as quickly as you can.
   3. Write down bizarre ideas — they might trigger better ideas.
   4. Piggy back new ideas on previous ones.

Find out from professional video ad makers what they do (4)

Get Toy Co. support to make video ad for them (6)

Talk with Mary Jane about being my partner to make video ad (5)

Look at good (award winning) video ads (3) (7)

**Major Goal to Accomplish:**
To move from print advertising to video advertising

Keep mentor apprised of my progress on these action steps (1)

Get Boss' support for me to do a video ad

Read books on video advertising to gain knowledge base, learn "jargon", etc. (2)

4a 5a 6a 7a — Get mentor's coaching before I talk with Boss, Toy Co., Mary Jane, etc.

**More Directions before leaving this page:**

1. **Explain** to your partner why you proposed what you did above.
2. **Jointly decide** what should be done first, second, third, etc. — then Protege writes 1, 2, 3, etc. to indicate the **rank order** of each idea.
3. **Go to page 3** to develop an Action Plan. ⟶

## Example of: *Mentoring Action Plan* [MAP]

<u>NOTES:</u>

- Below is part of the *Mentoring Action Plan* my Protege (Elaine) and I created from the Ideas we had *brainstormed*.

- The #1 attached to each **Action Step** indicates that she kept me apprised of her <u>progress</u> on each Action Step.

- Notice that she got **Coaching** from me <u>before</u> talking with Mary Jane (to become her partner to make the Video Ad), with the Toy Company (to get them as a client for the Video Ad), and with her Boss (to get his support).

- This *MAP* illustrates that the Mentor can *Arrange for Other Help* from secondary Mentors, in addition to directly providing help.

- Always prepare your Protege <u>before</u> he or she meets with <u>secondary</u> Mentors who can *Provide Other Help* (agree on questions to ask and what to look for and learn; provide coaching if necessary, like I did before Elaine talked with her Boss to get his support).

- Have your Protege report back to you as the <u>primary</u> Mentor – what was done and learned. Discuss how this will help achieve the Protege's Goal.

| Protege Goal to achieve: |
|---|

| Dates<br>(timeframe) | Logically-sequenced Action Steps for achieving Protege Goal<br>(Consists of Protege activities plus help Mentor & other resources will provide) |
|---|---|
| | Keep Mentor apprised of my progress on each Action Step. #1 |
| | Read books on video advertising to gain Knowledge Base (jargon, etc.). +#1 |
| | Look at award winning Video Ads. +#1 |
| | Find out from Professional video ad makers what they do. +#1 |
| | Get Mentor's coaching before talking with Mary Jane, Toy Co., Boss. #5 |
| | Talk with Mary Jane about being my partner to make Video Ad. +#1 |

**NOTE:** This Transcript does not adequately portray everything that took place as I helped Elaine. ***Mentoring for Results* Training Video** shows how Elaine's body language changed as she finally decided to transition into video advertising. And *transformed*: became aware of what to do and how, gained needed confidence, and gradually became fully committed to take action – after she had waffled and agonized for over two years because of her fear of failure.

You can view this video by accessing my online course. View **PROMO** at:

https://graysacademy.teachable.com/p/mentor-one-another-advanced-training

**Summarized Tips for Mentors:**
1. Understand how a person functions at each *Level of Awareness & Competence* – so you can equip a protege to progress from Levels 1-2 to 3.
2. Identify a protege who has a challenging situation. Employ Mentoring Style Flexibility while using the 6-Step Mentoring Process to help this protege progress to the Consciously Competent Level to handle this situation.
3. Efficiently guide the protege from Step 1 to 2, etc. so this Process doesn't "drag on.." Ask: "Are you ready for the next Step?" to prompt "moving on."
4. Do NOT: "tell protege what to do" or "expect protege to figure out what to do" on his/her own.
5. Read body language cues to get useful feedback (like I did).
6. Re-read the *Transcript* (M-9, M-10, M-27, M-30, M-39, M-40) and note *when* and *why* I "asked permission" to employ particular mentoring behaviors. Remember to "ask permission" of your protege, and read body language cues to see the positive, receptive reaction.


**Summarized Tips for Proteges:**
1. Make sure you understand how a person functions at each *Level of Awareness & Competence.* Remember this: many proteges are initially functioning at Level 1 or 2 when they encounter a challenging situation. They (and you?) mostly need equipping to reach Level 3.
2. Remember: Do not "get stuck" wanting only your most preferred Mentoring Style and behaviors to be provided (e.g., Elaine twice requested *Advice*).
3. If you tend to resist certain kinds of mentor assistance, or become defensive, tell your mentor to "ask permission" before employing these behaviors.


**Summarized Tips for Coordinators & Champions:**
1. Ensure an Expert trains mentor-protege partners to employ Mentoring Style Flexibility and the 6-Step Mentoring Process.
2. Monitor whether mentors are employing those Mentoring Styles/behaviors most commonly used during each Step of the 6-Step Mentoring Process.
3. Make sure mentors help proteges reach the Consciously Competent Level to handle a particular situation – without "telling them what to do" or "expecting them to figure out what to do"
4. Order my *Mentoring for Results Training Video* and use it to train mentor-protege partners. (You can stop it at key points and lead a discussion to engage viewer's thinking about what they might do, and why.)
5. To conduct Partner Training, order my *Mentoring for Results Workbook* and *training materials* to enhance mentoring relationships and benefits.

#####

# Chapter 5

## Proven Mentoring Assessments
## Enhance Mentor-Protege *Compatibility & Benefits*

In Chapter 5, I describe ***Mentoring Assessments*** that have enhanced over 20,000 *formalized* mentoring relationships – and can be used for matching "best-fit" mentoring partners in ONE day. These Assessments are not used during *informal* mentoring:

1. ***Mentoring Style Indicator***.

2. ***Protege Needs Inventory***.

3. ***General Style of Functioning Indicator***.

➢ ***One-Day Partner Matching Process*** using these Mentoring Assessments.

At the front of this book, John Murphy endorsed the impact of my Mentoring Assessments – which I repeat here – because John personally knows their beneficial impact. He oversaw and participated in two formalized mentoring programs I helped two organizations plan and implement over a ten year period.

> "William Gray has produced an epic work on formalized mentoring relationships that work. Bill's work is significant in breaking new ground for understanding the importance of the journey for both the mentor and protege to succeed. Equally important are the tools provided to guide both parties. These tools are like road-signs or directions on a GPS. They guide you to the right destination with the fewest delays. Bill is responsible for my personal success as a mentor, at two organizations (**Air National Guard** and **Defense Supply Center Columbus**) where I helped introduce the formalized mentoring program concept."
>
> ~**John Murphy**, Retired Lieutenant Colonel USAF, and former Change Manager, Defense Supply Center Columbus, Ohio.

According to lots of research, there is NO "ideal" mentor with all the people skills, time, experience, and expertise that a particular protege needs. There is NO "ideal" protege (or mentee), who will accept the various types of assistance a particular mentor can provide.

But, there are "real" tools for enhancing mentor-protege relationships and benefits – the Mentoring Assessments described below.

*1. Mentoring Style Indicator*

**enhances Mentor-Protege Relationships**

Chapter 1 described how to:

1) Answer the *MSI Situations* (as PROTEGE or MENTOR).

2) **Calculate** scores.

3) **Graph** your and your partner's **Profiles**.

4) Discuss **Interpretations** of both Profiles

5) **Answer  Questions** to enhance your mentoring relationship.

The *Mentoring Style Indicator* can be used to perform **One-Day Partner Matching** of compatible mentor-protege partners

[described at the end of this chapter]

Match partners with *MSI* scores that are similar enough they won't clash, but not so similar/identical that partners cannot learn from one another.

- When scores are in the **Moderate/Balanced Profile** range – or just outside this range – partners are most likely to work together harmoniously.

Even thought there are NO "ideal" mentor-protege partners, it is best NOT to match partners with these extremely different (opposite) Profiles:

- *Preferred Mentoring Styles* should not be extremely different (opposite), such as a mentor who scores 23 or 24 on Informational Mentoring Style and a protege who scores 23o 24 on Confirming Mentoring Style. This mentor strongly prefers *equipping*, whereas this protege strongly wants *empowering*. They are extreme opposites who are likely to clash.

- Similarly, do not match a mentor who strongly prefers *empowering* with a protege who strongly wants *equipping* – or vice versa – to prevent clashing.

When I train mentor-protege partners, I encourage them to function at the ***Consciously Competent Level***: consciously employ *less-preferred* Mentoring Styles so they develop *Mentoring Style Flexibility* as a competency – and can engage in ***Situational Mentoring***.

I encourage partners to re-answer the ***MSI*** 5-6 months into their mentoring relationship to find out if their *Preferred Mentoring Style Profiles* have changed:

- o Highest scores should now be lower.
- o Lowest scores should now be higher.
- o This indicates a preference for *Mentoring Style Flexibility*.
- o When all scores fall in the **Moderate** range, this indicates a ***Balanced Profile*** so that mentors provide all 4 Mentoring Styles/behaviors and proteges are receptive to this. These relationships are very successful.

#####

## *2. Protege Needs Inventory*
## enhances Mentor-Protege Relationships

During formalized mentoring, mentors help proteges satisfy important Needs as Goals that are achieved. When I first started training mentor-protege partners, they engaged in a Goal Setting Activity. Most partners spent this time "talking about" issues, challenges, hopes, bosses, personal experiences, etc. – without identifying a Goal to achieve.

So, I developed different versions of the ***Protege Needs Inventory*** [PNI] so that:

- ➢ Proteges answer the *PNI* to quickly identify important *Needs* to achieve as Goals.

- ➢ Mentors answer the *PNI* to quickly identify *Expertise* that matches the protege's important *Needs*.

- ➢ Partners create a ***Mentoring Action Plan*** to achieve a protege Goal that the mentor had corresponding Expertise to provide.

Below are *excerpts* from different versions
of the ***Protege Needs Inventory***.

---

***PNI for New Hires***

**Section I. Adjusting to the New Job**

**[excerpts from 57 Needs Statements]**

---

2. Learning to work effectively with other people, especially on a team.

6. Understanding the company's structure and the protege's position in it.

9. Maintaining one's personal integrity/diversity while "fitting in" with corporate norms.

10. Gathering and organizing relevant information before meeting with protege's manager.

25. Overcoming the inadequacies of previous education and/or training.

---

***PNI for Career Development***

**Section IV. Handling Specific Situations**

**[excerpts from 67 Needs Statements]**

---

1. Seeking and accepting feedback for self-improvement without defensiveness.

9. Modifying protege's style to be appropriate for different situations.

14. "Reading" people's behavior that occurs in group dynamics.

16. Conducting productive meetings.

18. making clear, precise presentations.

---

***PNI for Leaders***

**Section IV. Leading a Major Paradigm Shift**

**[excerpts from 52 Needs Statements]**

---

1. Anticipating changing customer needs that will force a paradigm shift.

2. Innovating new products or services to meet these customer needs.

3. Championing needed change & enlisting others in its pursuit.

9. Recognizing the need for change & removing barriers.

#####

### *3. General Style of Functioning*

## enhances Mentor-Protege Relationships

There are many well-known Personality Assessments, which have in common these characteristics:

- Have **VALIDITY** in "measuring what they purport to measure."
- Are **RELIABLE** in consistently giving the 'same' Profile when re-answered.

I developed the ***General Style of Functioning Indicator*** some 30 years ago for different reasons:

- Other assessments "type-cast" you because they were designed to identify a stable Profile that should not change over time. These assessments "reliably" identify the "same" profile when re-answered. This is why they were created.

- My clients needed an accurate Profile assessment that identified "where you're at" so that you could "change" and "develop flexibility" because of training and subsequent "conscious effort" to do this – so you can communicate, interact and work better with others.

- Such "flexibility" is essential today because nearly everyone works on Project Teams, where members must be different to solve problems, create innovative products, serve customers who are "different" from them. [A basketball team with 5 7-foot Centers cannot beat a team comprised of "5 position" players: shooting & point Guards + weak & strong Forwards + 7-foot Center.]

- To develop the ***GSF Indicator***, I used the same Dimensions that many other Personality Assessments use – as illustrated below:

  - Task-oriented or People-oriented.

  - Extrovert or Introvert.

- ◇ **Prevent clashes with a diagonally opposite Style:**
  - ○ Feeling Style **and** Results Style
  - ○ Analytic Style **and** Creative Style
- ◇ **Better teammate for projects.**
- ◇ **Can interact better with anyone.**
- ◇ **Better Person-Career Fit.**
- ◇ **Examples:**
  - ○ **Husband & wife**
  - ○ **Turner Construction**
  - ○ **Shell Oil**

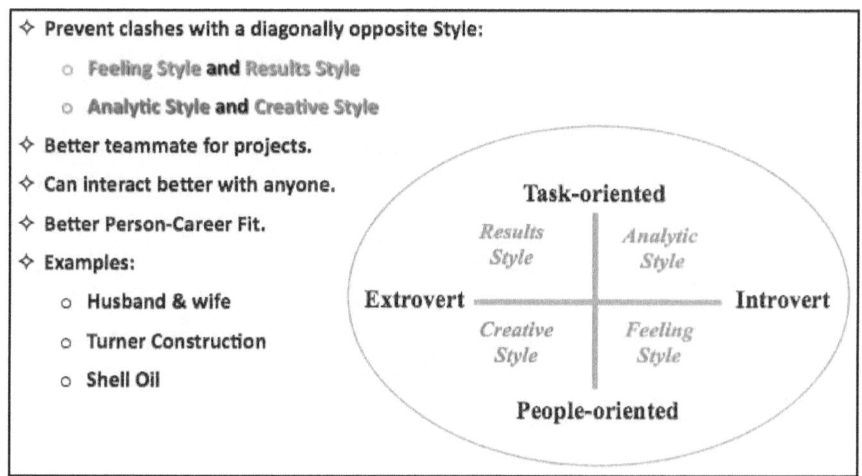


## Identify *Your* General Style of Functioning
[excerpts from the GSF Indicator]

### Directions:

1) Read all 4 Statements inside each Table (before going to the next Table).

2) Under RANK put "4" beside that Statement that is MOST like you.

3) Under RANK put "1" beside that Statement that is LEAST like you.

4) RANK other Statements that are more like you ("3") or less like you ("2").

| Statements  (Group 1) | Style | RANK |
|---|---|---|
| I want only essential information so I'm not mired in details. | **R** | |
| I want lots of factual evidence to be certain before acting. | **A** | |
| I want to influence people by telling them my creative ideas. | **C** | |
| I want my feelings and concerns to influence people. | **F** | |

| Statements  (Group 2) | Style | RANK |
|---|---|---|
| I want to complete tasks quickly and effectively. | **R** | |
| I want enough time to carry out tasks correctly. | **A** | |
| I want to change those things I think need changing. | **C** | |
| I want people to consider how work tasks affect other people. | **F** | |

| Statements  (Group 3) | Style | RANK |
|---|---|---|
| I act quickly to produce desired outcomes. | R | |
| I act cautiously to avoid stupid mistakes. | A | |
| I make decisions quickly, to implement my innovative ideas. | C | |
| I act after carefully considering other people's feelings. | F | |

| Statements  (Group 4) | Style | RANK |
|---|---|---|
| I act in a goal-oriented manner. | R | |
| I act in a logical manner. | A | |
| I act on my gut-level hunches. | C | |
| I act in a dependable manner. | F | |

| Statements  (Group 5) | Style | RANK |
|---|---|---|
| I need to get work done that produces desired results. | R | |
| I need people to respect my ability to do high quality work. | A | |
| I need recognition for innovative ideas to feel good about myself. | C | |
| I need to feel appreciated as a person to feel good about myself. | F | |

| Statements  (Group 6) | Style | RANK |
|---|---|---|
| I need to accomplish major goals to feel valued. | R | |
| I need to complete specific tasks based on my logical thinking. | A | |
| I need other people to acknowledge each new project I start. | C | |
| I need to feel valued for being myself as I work. | F | |

| Statements  (Group 7) | Style | RANK |
|---|---|---|
| I enjoy reading Executive Summaries. | R | |
| I enjoy reading and comparing lots of research studies. | A | |
| I enjoy starting new projects. | C | |
| I enjoy interacting with teammates while doing projects. | F | |

| Statements  (Group 8) | Style | RANK |
|---|---|---|
| I like quickly completing what I start. | R | |
| I like comparing and contrasting facts and ideas. | A | |
| I like originating new ideas and then expressing them. | C | |
| I like discussing people's feelings and concerns. | F | |

## Calculate Your *General Style of Functioning*

### Directions:

1) In each Row, write down the RANK (4,3,2,1) you gave to each General Style (R, A, C, F) for each Group of Statements above.

2) Add your scores in each Column, to calculate your Total Score for R,A,C,F.

3) Write down your Total Score for each General Style.

| Statements | R=Results Style | A=Analytic Style | C=Creative Style | F=Feeling Style |
|---|---|---|---|---|
| Group 1 | | | | |
| Group 2 | | | | |
| Group 3 | | | | |
| Group 4 | | | | |
| Group 5 | | | | |
| Group 7 | | | | |
| Group 7 | | | | |
| Group 8 | | | | |
| Total Score = | | | | |

## Graph Your General Style of Functioning
## PROFILE

## Directions:

1)   In each Row, write down the **Total Score** for each General Style.

2)   Highest Total Score(s) indicate *your **Preferred** General Style of Functioning* (could be a single Style, or 2 or more Styles).

| Graphed PROFILE of Preferred General Style of Functioning | | | |
|---|---|---|---|
| **STYLES** | **WEAK** | **MODERATE** | **STRONG** |
| **Results** | 8 9 10 11 12 13 14 | 15 16 17 18 19 20 21 22 23 24 25 | 26 27 28 29 30 31 32 |
| **Analytic** | 8 9 10 11 12 13 14 | 15 16 17 18 19 20 21 22 23 24 25 | 26 27 28 29 30 31 32 |
| **Creative** | 8 9 10 11 12 13 14 | 15 16 17 18 19 20 21 22 23 24 25 | 26 27 28 29 30 31 32 |
| **Feeling** | 8 9 10 11 12 13 14 | 15 16 17 18 19 20 21 22 23 24 25 | 26 27 28 29 30 31 32 |

## Answer these Questions:

- What is your *most preferred* General Style? *Least preferred*?

- Do you agree with this assessment of your Profile? Why? Why not?

- Which General Styles do you most clash with? Diagonal opposites? Why?

- Think of actual persons who clash with you. Would you guess their preferred General Style is diagonally opposite to your most preferred General Style? How do you know this?

Most people score high on 2 or 3 General Styles. This means they know something personal about these Styles – and thus know how to interact, communicate and work with people whose scores are even higher (because they have a stronger preference for these particular Styles).

Diagonal opposite Styles – **Results-Feeling** and **Analytic-Creative** – tend to 'attract' because their differences are intriguing, but also 'clash' most often. Read their defining characteristics to understand why.

<table>
<tr><td>

**Results Style:**

- Task-oriented & Extroverted
- Quickly decides with little information
- Goal-oriented & expects this of others
- Multi-tasks ("busy")
- Views "off-topic" discussion as wasteful
- Can be "bossy" & impatient
- Gets the job done
- Works quickly
- Not easily distracted

</td><td>

**Analytic Style:**

- Task-oriented & Introverted
- Slowly decides using lots of information – "wants to be sure"
- Is "overloaded' if too many tasks or not enough time
- "Paralysis because of analysis"
- Quality-oriented while doing tasks
- Cannot multi-task ("focuses")
- Needs respect for logical analysis
- Critical eye sees mistakes
- Avoids "stupidity"

</td></tr>
<tr><td>

**Creative Style:**

- Extroverted & People-oriented
- Quickly decides using gut-level hunches, intuition, impulse
- Desires variation & innovative changes
- Multi-tasks (starts lots of projects)
- Dislikes restrictions / rules
- High energy, moves around
- Likes to talk & persuade others
- Needs lots of recognition

</td><td>

**Feeling Style:**

- People-oriented & Introverted
- Concerned about feelings (own & other people's)
- Wants to be emotionally understood & included
- Less concerned with job getting done
- Values harmony (seems likeable)
- Can be passive-aggressive
- Needs to be "listened to"
- Loyal when supported / affirmed

</td></tr>
</table>

## Overcome Clashing by "Style-shifting"

[*Consciously Competent* in developing *General Style Flexibility*]

To prevent clashing, don't be matched with a "diagonally opposite" partner whose extremely high score is the *opposite* of your extremely high score.

To overcome clashing, learn how to "Style-shift" by consciously developing **General Style Flexibility** as a competency. Below are two actual client examples.

**At Shell Oil Company** (in Miri, on the Island of Borneo):

Nearly all of the 300 mentors preferred a **Results-oriented Style**. These ex-pats from the Netherlands and UK tended to issue strong directives and "boss" indigenous workers to produce better results.

Nearly all of their 300 indigenous proteges preferred a **Feeling-oriented Style**. They valued harmony and getting along with others because of their culture. So, they pretended to "go along to get along" with "bossy" ex-pats: they passively submitted publicly to ex-pat's strong directives, but then disagreed behind the scenes, often aggressively sabotaging directives (this is called the *passive aggressive syndrome*).

After we provided instruction on the characteristics of each General Style, we created small groups comprised of mentors-and-proteges, so that all 4 Preferred General Styles of Functioning were represented in each group.

Each group listed specific ways *their* preferred Style needed to change to work better with the other 3 Styles.

Each group listed how the *other* 3 Styles needed to change to work better with their preferred Style.

Each group role-played "Style-shifting" – amidst much laughter – because actual situations were "acted out" to illustrate actual "Style clashes." This laughter relieved the pressure that had built up over many years.

This training activity enabled mentor-and-protege partners to consciously "Style-shift" instead of clashing.

At **Turner Construction Company** (America's largest and fastest growing construction company):

I conducted Partner Training so the proteges (NEW project managers and leaders) learned how to work harmoniously with architects, bankers, and politicians.

All 100 proteges were ***results-oriented***. Mentors helped them develop a different General Style of working, thinking, valuing, and communicating so they could work harmoniously with:

- ***creative*** architects, who frequently changed designs with little concern for added cost and time;
- ***analytical*** bankers and estimators, who questioned all costs for everything;
- ***feeling-oriented*** politicians, who wanted to win emotional approval from voters, by addressing their concerns about the environment, disruption to citizens to make space for new construction, and hiring local people (especially the unemployed) for the project.

Prior to this Partner Training, all proteges valued being only *results-oriented*: they believed "build it on time and on budget" was the key to success. They learned that consciously "Style-shifting" as a new competency is the key to success – to work well with others.

## One-Day **Partner Matching**

For some clients – e.g., Kaiser Permanente, Florida Power & Light, W.R. Grace and others – I facilitated **One-Day Partner Matching** that saved hundreds of hours matching mentoring partners, compared to conventional methods (resumes; applications; interviews).

The Coordinator invites already-identified proteges (20-25 for the Pilot Program) and potential mentors (3-5 more than the number of proteges so there are "more mentors to choose from").


Below is a typical Agenda I facilitate. The Coordinator(s) and Planning Team should be present – to observe potential partners interacting, so they can match actual partners at the end of the day.

**1<sup>st</sup> Overview Program Requirements.**

**2<sup>nd</sup> Overview the Partner Matching process.**

**3<sup>rd</sup> Overview Partner Training** to occur next day.

**4<sup>th</sup> Compare *Preferred General Style of Functioning*:**

1) All mentors and proteges answer our ***GSF*** assessment to identify *Preferred General Style*.

2) I explain defining characteristics of the *4 General Styles* [see *GSF* Diagram].

3) I arrange proteges to rotate through mentors.

4) Each mentor explains his/her Most and Least Preferred General Style to each protege.

5) Each protege explains his/her Most and Least Preferred General Style to each mentor

6) Rotations occur every 5 minutes, so each potential "M-P pair" has to stay on task

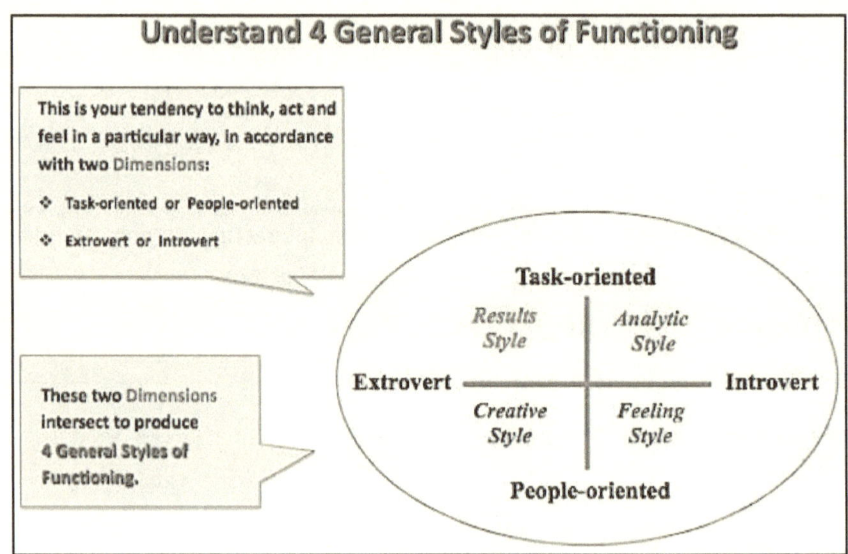


**5th Compare *Preferred Mentoring Styles*:**

1) All mentors and proteges answer our ***Mentoring Style Indicator*** assessment to identify *Preferred Mentoring Style*.

2) I explain the *4 Mentoring Styles* and behaviors [see Chapter 1-3].

3) I arrange proteges to rotate through mentors.

4) Each mentor explains his/her Most and Least Preferred Mentoring Style to each protege.

5) Each protege explains his/her Most and Least Preferred Mentoring Style to each mentor.

6) Rotations occur every 5 minutes, so each potential "M-P pair" has to stay on task.

**6th Compare Needs and Expertise:**

1) All mentors identify their Expertise and proteges identify their Needs by answering our ***Protege Needs Inventory***.

2) I arrange proteges to rotate through mentors.

3) Each protege explains his/her 5 or 6 most important Needs.

4) Each mentor explains corresponding Expertise.

5) Rotations occur every 5 minutes, so each potential "M-P pair" has to stay on task.

**7$^{th}$ Nominate 3 Partners You can Work With & Explain Why** – I explain this final activity and how written nominations will be used to match Mentor-Protege Partners for tomorrow's Partner Training. Unless notified NOT to attend, everyone is expected to attend and participate in our *Mentoring for Results Partner Training*.

**8$^{th}$ Match Partners for Tomorrow's Partner Training** – after participants leave, Coordinator and Planning Team match best-fit partners using Nomination Forms; I answer questions about whether these Partners are compatible on *General Style Preference* and compatible on *Mentoring Style Preference*.

**9$^{th}$ Notify non-selected Mentors** – Coordinator and Planning Team notify the "3-5 extra mentors" NOT to attend tomorrow's Partner Training, thank them for participating today, and encourage them to volunteer again.

## How Effective and Efficient are Other Methods of Partner Matching?

Researchers have consistently found that a committed Mentoring Committee needs 3-5 *people hours* to match each PAIR of mentor-protege partners – using paper-based methods:
- Written applications.
- Custom-made forms.
- Resumes.

No one really knows how ***compatible*** these matches are. Typically, 10-20% feel so *mis-matched* that they request to be re-matched with another partner.

***Coca-Cola*'s story:**
After losing a discrimination lawsuit, the Consent Decree required ***Coca-Cola*** to match mentor-protege partners throughout the USA for the next 5-6 years – until everyone who wanted to participate in a *formalized* mentoring program, was matched and participated in this mentoring program. Everything had to be documented!

- The initial matching required "400 *people hours* to match 100 PAIRS of mentor-protege partners" [=40,000 total hours]. [Can you imagine the cost?]

- To perform faster and more precise matching, Coca-Cola licensed our **Web-based Matching System** because "we must do best-fit matching several times per year, for the next 5-6 years." [Can you appreciate the savings?]

**Summarized Tips for Mentors & Proteges:**
1. Use the *Mentoring Assessments* described in this chapter and book to: (1) identify your characteristics; (2) identify characteristics of your actual or potential partner; (3) discuss this information to enhance a "best-fit" partnership.
2. Order these *Mentoring Assessments* and other mentoring materials via email: **wgray@mentoring-solutions.com**.

**Summarized Tips for Coordinators & Champions:**
1. Contact me to conduct ONE-DAY Partner Matching – to save you lots of time and money, and create "best-fit" matches.
2. My ***Mentoring for Results Trainer's Guide*** describes how to use these proven *Mentoring Assessments* during Partner Training – so partners develop good relationships.
3. Make sure an ***EXPERT** in Partner Trainer* uses these Mentoring Assessments to ***Enhance Mentoring Relationships & Benefits***.

#####

# Chapter 6

## *Formalized* Mentoring Satisfies Protege Needs/Goals better than *Informal* Mentoring

**In Chapter 6, you'll learn:**

➢ How *informal* "do-your-own-thing" mentoring relationships develop and tend to end badly. This did not occur in 150 *formalized* mentoring programs I've helped to develop!

➢ How *formalized* mentoring overcomes 10 shortcomings of *informal* mentoring.

### *Informal* Mentoring

Over 300 books on mentoring have been published, over 1,000 articles have been written, and over 500 Master's Theses and Doctoral Dissertations have been completed. About 90% of everything written on mentoring describes *informal* mentoring:

❖ How *informal* mentoring "spontaneously happens" when a mentor is attracted to a protege because of "special chemistry."

❖ How lucky proteges are "chosen" to receive *informal* mentoring, typically without knowing this is happening for months.

❖ How this *informal relationship* develops over time (5-8 years or longer).

❖ The many benefits gained by "chosen" proteges (e.g., better first job; faster advancement; higher salary).

❖ How *informal* mentoring often ends badly.

Two best-selling books, Gail Sheehy's *Passages* (1976) and Daniel Levinson's *Seasons of a Man's Life* (1978), are often credited with popularizing *informal* mentoring and focusing attention and subsequent research on the nature of the *informal* mentoring relationship and the benefits produced for proteges.

Why were these two books so influential? Sheehy found that 100% of the women she interviewed credited the assistance of *informal* mentors for helping them successfully navigate major life passages. Levinson found that 100% of the men he interviewed reached the highest levels in their organization because *informal* mentors fulfilled the *Mentoring Roles* illustrated in the schematic.

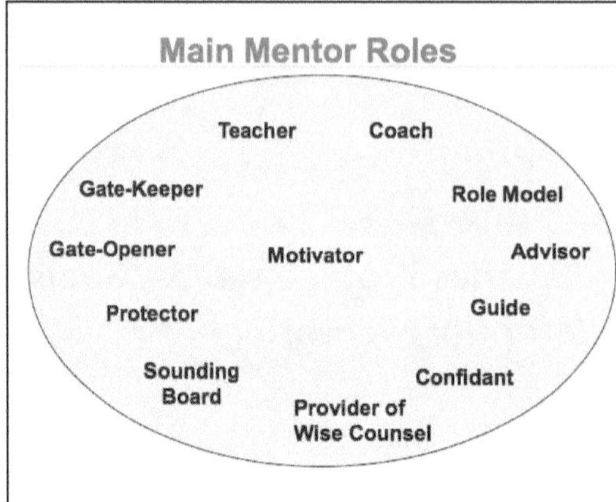


Informal mentors advance protege careers by fulfilling these *Mentor Roles*:

***Sponsor:*** recommends proteges for special assignments that showcase their particular talents.

***Advocate:*** speaks favorably about proteges to enhance their reputations in the eyes of key decision-makers.

Linda Phillips-Jones was the first person to research the developmental stages through which *informal* mentoring relationships progress. Her findings were published as the first dissertation on mentoring. (Linda Lee Phillips. *Mentors and proteges: A study of the career development of women managers and executives in business and industry*. Doctoral Dissertation. UCLA, 1977).

Below are the **five developmental stages** of *informal* mentoring she discovered:

1. **Initiation:** mentor chooses protege (usually without protege knowing this).
2. **The Sparkle:** mutual admiration occurs.
3. **Development:** partners recognize each other's shortcomings.
4. **Parting:** protege seeks independence (usually involves a *power struggle*).
5. **Transformation:** become colleagues if Parting is good.

[Also see: Linda Phillips-Jones. *Mentors and Proteges: How to Succeed with the New Mentoring Partnerships*. Coalition of Counseling Centers.]

Kathy Kram's 1980 dissertation study validated this progression from one stage to another during *informal* mentoring, and what occurs during this progression. However, she gave her **four developmental stages** different names:

1. **Initiation:** includes being chosen by the mentor and admiring one another.
2. **Cultivation:** involves gaining trust and mutual respect for each other's accomplishments.
3. **Separation:** often hurtful when the protege seeks independence.
4. **Redefinition of the relationship:** perhaps as colleagues and friends.

Both of these often-cited dissertation studies found that *informal* mentor-protege relationships usually begin with the mentor choosing the protege, often without the protege knowing that mentoring is being provided.

Then, a "honeymoon" period occurs during which the partners fail to see shortcomings in each other, followed by the development of a reality-based relationship.

Sometimes, problems occur as the more competent and confident protege wants to leave the relationship, and be perceived by the mentor in a new way: as a colleague or friend.

Kram's research also contributed new knowledge about two main types of *informal* mentoring assistance that proteges seek out and accept: **male proteges** want *career* assistance that advances one's career, whereas **female proteges** want *psychosocial* assistance that provides nurturance.

Kram identified five **Career Functions** that *informal* mentors provide for **male proteges**:

- o **Sponsorship** for special assignments and career advancement.
- o **Coaching** on how to perform in particular situations.
- o **Exposure and visibility** when the protege was seen with the mentor.
- o **Protection** as the protege risked trying something that did not work out.
- o **Challenging work assignments** that showcase the protege's talents.

Kram identified four **Psychosocial Functions** that *informal* mentors provide for **female proteges**:

- o **Acceptance and confirmation** of the protege as a person.
- o **Counseling** for difficult situations.
- o **Role modeling** what to do in particular situations.
- o **Friendship** and socializing together.

[For more details, see: Kathy E. Kram. *Mentoring at Work: Developmental Relationships in Organizational Life.* Scott, Foresman & Co., 1985. ]

Subsequent researchers of *informal* mentoring also found that male proteges seek out career-oriented mentoring to aid career development and advancement, whereas female proteges seek out psychosocial mentoring to be nurtured and supported.

This Career or Psychosocial preference can be prevented within a *formalized* mentoring program by **teaching** mentoring partners the importance of both types of mentor assistance – and then **training** mentor-protege partners to employ mentoring concepts, models and assessment tools described throughout this book.

### *"Announcements"* and *"Initiatives"*
### FAIL to produce Expected Benefits for
### Proteges, Mentors & their Organizations

Oftentimes, well-meaning mentoring proponents within an organization (or hired consultants from outside) will make a simple "**Announcement**" to encourage "do-your-own-thing" *Informal* Mentoring. Or, will partially plan a Mentoring "**Initiative**" where all essential components for effective mentoring have *not* been defined and designed to ensure intended outcomes and benefits are produced.

These efforts fail, when compared to a *formalized* mentoring program where all essential components are thoughtfully *defined* and *designed* and then *delivered* to satisfy business purposes (the "business case") and produce intended benefits for individual proteges, for their mentors, and for the sponsoring organization.

Over 75% of the contracts we get from organizations are to help them develop a *formalized* mentoring program that works, after they have tried implementing simple "Announcements" or partially-planned "Initiatives" that were launched by *Non-experts* **in Mentoring Program Development**.

## Comparison of
## *Informal* vs. *Formalized* Mentoring

The Table below summarizes major differences that distinguish *Informal* **Mentoring** from *Formalized* **Mentoring** (that typically occurs within a *Formalized* Mentoring Program).

| M=Mentor P=Protege | Summary of Major Differences | |
|---|---|---|
| | *Informal Mentoring* | *Formalized Mentoring* |
| **1. How it Starts** | Spontaneously, naturally | Carefully planned |
| **2. Duration** | Longer (3-5 years or more) | Shorter (4–36 months) |
| **3. Structure** | Whatever happens "happens" | Guidelines & expectations |
| **4. How M-P meet** | Mentor usually chooses protege | Coordinator matches partners; can self-match with partner |
| **5. M-P Bonding** | Requires "special chemistry" | Based on commitment |
| **6. Goals** | Arise during mentoring | Specified at beginning & during |
| **7. Training** | None; do whatever you want | Training teaches what to do |
| **8. M-P Meetings** | Happen when needed | Regularly scheduled |
| **9. Monitoring** | None – entirely on own | Coordinator regularly monitors |
| **10. Protege Benefits** | Career advancement sponsored | Develop talent & competencies |

# How *Formalized* Mentoring
# Overcomes Shortcomings of *Informal* Mentoring

## 1. How mentoring starts:

Typically, *informal* mentoring starts spontaneously or naturally when a mentor notices a capable person and begins providing assistance, often without the protege knowing this for several months. Male mentors often choose a protege like themselves (another male) because this is more comfortable and outcomes are more predictable. Historically, this "old boys network" excluded females and minorities.

Because *informally* mentored proteges benefit more than their non-mentored peers, *formalized* mentoring programs were started in the late 1970s to include and benefit everyone – especially women and minorities, who were typically not chosen to receive *informal* mentoring at that time.

Over 80% of the 150 *formalized* mentoring programs I've helped to develop since 1978 were started to support Equal Employment Opportunity or Affirmative Action or Diversity Initiatives. To do this, mentoring partners are **intentionally matched** so the mentor and protege are not alike on demographics like gender, ethnicity, age, function, position, department. This enables partners to learn how to work with someone who is different, and then transfer this knowledge to work more comfortably and effectively with anyone in the diversified workforce.

The most successful *formalized* mentoring occurs within a thoughtfully planned and structured *formalized* program that has a designated starting date and end date, so partners know how long they are committing to work together. A successful program is started to benefit a particular type of protege for a particular business purpose (e.g., orienting new hires and helping them get up to speed faster; exploring career path options so the right one is chosen; developing core competencies in future leaders for succession planning).

To ensure *formalized* mentoring relationships start off well, a program coordinator carefully matches the right partners so that mentor expertise matches protege needs. Such matching enables partners to quickly focus on what they will work on together. Proteges will not benefit much by being matched with a mentor who cannot help them. Matching the right partners is essential for achieving the intended goals of a *formalized* mentoring program. I've found that mis-matched partners don't become more compatible when trained, or when a trained program coordinator provides extra assistance.

## 2. Duration:

*Informal* mentoring typically lasts for 3 to 5 years, and sometimes even longer (e.g., Annie Sullivan mentored the deaf and blind Helen Keller from her childhood in 1887 until her death in 1936, nearly 50 years). Because it lasts so long, *informal* mentors have many opportunities to fulfill all those mentor roles and functions described previously, and this produces a more comprehensive impact on the protege than can occur in much shorter (6-36 months) *formalized* mentoring, where it is not possible to fulfill nearly so many roles and functions. Sometimes, after the *formalized* relationship ends, partners will continue meeting less formally.

## 3. How mentoring partners stay together:

Do you believe "special chemistry" is needed for mentoring success? If so, you've been influenced by *informal* mentoring. *Special chemistry* is needed to hold this type of relationship together over many years, whereas *formalized* mentoring is based on commitment to work together in a much shorter program.

I've also found that training mentor-protege *partners* together enables them to quickly develop a comfort level for discussing real issues during the training session, so that mentoring actually occurs there. When mentoring partners enter my **Mentoring for Results™ Partner Training**, I ask everyone "to raise a hand when I call out the number from 10 down to zero that indicates how well you already know your partner, where 10 indicates you know one another quite well already and zero indicates you don't know one another at all." As I count down the numbers, I hear a lot of nervous laughter – until I call out the lower numbers. This indicates that neither the mentor nor the protege knows one another very well.

They immediately feel more comfortable when I say: "It is because you don't know your partners very well that both of you are here together to learn about one another and how to develop a good mentoring relationship that achieves desired goals."

## 4. Structure:

Whatever happens in an *informal* mentoring relationship, "just happens" – that's why it is said to be spontaneous or natural. In contrast, *formalized* mentoring has well-defined and thoughtfully designed structures – such as Program Guidelines and Expectations – which are needed so mentoring partners know what to do and will do it.

I'll always remember collaboratively planning mentoring programs for Pillsbury and Pacific Bell (now called Telesis), when we agreed that mentors would not provide any coaching of needed skills because the proteges' supervisors had been trained to do this and would not support the mentoring program if mentors provided skill coaching. So, one Program Guideline stated: "If proteges need skill coaching to improve performance, refer them to their supervisor to get this." Another important Guideline was mentioned earlier: "Mentors must not be an Advocate or Sponsor for protege advancement, because this could cause non-participants to undermine or sabotage the program."

Another important Guideline is to "Create and carry out an agreed upon Mentoring Action Plan for each protege goal to be achieved." You will learn why as you continue reading.

## 5. Goals:

In an *informal* mentoring relationship, protege goals emerge naturally or spontaneously throughout the duration of the relationship. In a much shorter *formalized* program, partners are typically matched so that mentor expertise matches protege needs. This enables mentors to help proteges quickly satisfy their needs by achieving desired goals. As mentioned previously, these programs are very goal-oriented: each program typically targets a particular type of protege for a particular purpose (e.g., orienting new hires and helping them get up to speed faster; exploring career path options so the right one is chosen; developing core competencies in future leaders for succession planning).

When I first began training mentor-protege partners, they did a goal-setting activity to identify what they would work on. I discovered that too many mentoring partners talked for 30-45 minutes without identifying any goals to achieve. This led me to develop different versions of a ***Protege Needs Inventory*** (*PNI*) for different types of proteges, purposes, and situations:

❖ For business and government situations, I developed three versions of the *PNI:* for orienting new hires, for aiding career development, and for developing leaders.

❖ For education situations: I developed three versions of the *PNI:* for inducting new teachers, for preparing new school administrators, and for assisting freshmen to succeed academically and stay in college.

Proteges answer the *PNI* to indicate their main needs, and mentors indicate their main expertise. During Partner Training, partners compare needs and expertise to agree on goals the mentor can help the protege achieve. In 1999, we converted the *PNI* into a web-based ***Needs-Expertise Inventory*** that instantly matches proteges with the right mentors, who can help them convert major needs into goals to be achieved.

## 6. Training:

There is none for *informal* mentoring. Consequently, mentoring partners "do their own thing." This is totally inappropriate in a much shorter *formalized* mentoring program, which is started to satisfy business purposes (e.g., reduce costly employee turnover; develop core competencies; support diversity initiatives) and to ensure proteges, mentors, and their organization benefit. If individual proteges don't achieve goals that align with the business purpose, there is no reason for starting the program. If mentors don't benefit in desired ways, they stop volunteering to share their time and expertise. If the organization doesn't benefit, it stops sponsoring the program.

It should be noted that **lack of training** was identified as the main reason for mentoring failures within corporations, in an eight-nation study reported by PA Personnel Services in 1986. To produce mutual benefits for proteges, mentors and their organization, I've found that *training partners together* produces better results than training only mentors or only proteges.

During our **Mentoring for Results™ Partner Training**, partners learn the same concepts and skills, and then immediately apply this so that mentoring actually takes place during partner training. Mentors have consistently said that what they learn and do together jump-starts the mentoring relationship by two to six months. Below is a brief description of key activities:

- o Partners identify the protege's major needs and mentor's corresponding expertise by answering our ***Protege Needs Inventory*** (or by answering the ***Needs-Expertise Inventory*** in our web-based Mentoring Management System®).
- o Partners quickly develop a comfort level that enables them to discuss real issues.
- o Partners compare their Preferred Mentoring Styles that they identified by answering the ***Mentoring Style Indicator***, and then use this so that the mentor (a) *equips* the protege with wisdom and practicum know-how, and *empowers* what the protege wants to learn, do, and become (described in Chapters 2-5).
- o Partners use a *6-Step Mentoring Process* to resolve an especially challenging issue (described in Chapter 4).
- o Partners create a *Mentoring Action Plan* for achieving an important protege goal.
- o Partners create a *Mentoring Partner Agreement* by answering 13 key questions, such as: Who will initiate meetings? What will you do if you lack time to get together as planned?

## 7. Mentor-protege meetings:

Because *informal* mentoring occurs spontaneously over many years, meetings are not as regularly scheduled, as they must be in a much shorter *formalized* mentoring program so that intended goals will be achieved. One of the common questions mentors ask before volunteering to participate in a *formalized* program is "How much time is required"? This is really a two-part question: (a) How many months? (b) How frequently do we meet? The answers are decided during Collaborative Program Planning, and are based on what a particular group of proteges needs to learn and do, and how much mentoring is needed to assist them.

Orienting new hires typically takes about 6 months, with meetings occurring once a week for one-to-two hours per month to get proteges up to speed. Developing future leaders requires 18-36 months, with meetings being scheduled by partners to fit the mentor's busy schedule (mentors are often at the highest levels: CEO, COO, CTO, etc. or Senior VPs).

The ***Mentoring Action Plan*** (MAP) that partners create during partner training ensures that (a) they agree on activities they will do together or separately, (b) they are both prepared for scheduled meetings, (c) they carry out agreed upon activities, and (d) they achieve the protege's goal for that Plan. Each MAP serves as a "roadmap" for achieving intended Goals because it converts Talk into Action Steps that produce intended Results.

## 8. Monitoring mentoring relationships and activity:

Mentoring partners might or might not do some kind of monitoring during *informal* mentoring while "doing their own thing." If they do, who knows what they monitor, and why: Whether the "special chemistry" is still there? Whether the mentor still has confidence in the protege to be successful, so the mentor will continue to provide assistance? What spontaneous goal has emerged and requires attention? How well partners are working together? Is it time to end the relationship?

In contrast, a trained mentoring program *coordinator* regularly monitors all aspects of *formalized* mentoring relationships to ensure mutual benefits are being produced for proteges, mentors, and their organization, because successful programs do not "run themselves." A trained coordinator knows what to monitor and what interventions to provide so small problems don't become big ones. From training over 300 coordinators, I've learned that they are the single most important person in successful programs.

Like a hovering helicopter, coordinators oversee the "big picture" they helped to create as participants during initial Collaborative Program Planning. Like a landed helicopter, they ensure the program is operating as planned, and mentoring partners feel well-matched and are achieving intended goals by creating and carrying out a Mentoring Action Plan (MAP) for each goal. The MAP provides a "roadmap" of where partners are going (the goal) and how they plan to get there (the action steps). Completed MAPs provide evidence of what partners did and learned, which is useful evidence for accountability and reporting to the sponsoring organization (or funding agency).

The cost of having a trained coordinator monitor all aspects of a *formalized* mentoring program is small compared to the multiple benefits produced by a successful program. For example, **Jet Propulsion Lab** (JPL) eventually had two full-time coordinators participate in program planning and then oversee publicity, facilitate partner matching, conduct partner training, provide regular monitoring, and perform formalized evaluation. They fulfilled these essential coordinator tasks for a series of different *formalized* mentoring programs – started initially just for new hires, then for their technical mentors who needed assistance with career development, and then for their mentors who wanted to transition into leadership positions. After *formalized* mentoring had progressed upward, through JPL's Technical Division, the Administrative Division did the same thing for its personnel at various levels.

Here is another example of the value of coordinators: Since 1992, **CSX Transportation** has had 8-15 coordinators on an Oversight Committee oversee 2-4 cycles of *formalized* mentoring each year in their Associate Development Program. Each coordinator is responsible for monitoring and assisting 2-to-6 pairs of mentoring partners (called Coaches and Associates, instead of mentors and proteges). The cost for this – including two days off-site to participate in my Mentoring for Results™ Partner Training – pales compared to the mutual benefits produced. Cross-functional mentoring that occurs between Labor and Management, and between different departments (like Sales and Finance), has produced better understanding and improved working relationships.

How? By breaking down traditional "silos" and resolving conflicts through increased understanding and appreciation of each other's roles and contributions. I remember one pair of mentoring partners from Sales and Finance who began with conflicting perceptions: "Do what it takes to get the sale" versus "We won't make money doing that." They eventually learned to respect each other's roles and contributions because they engaged in *reciprocal* mentoring. Then, they helped each other's departments learn the same things. You can imagine how this benefited CSX then, and subsequently.

Since 1992, CSX's mentors have benefited so much that they willingly serve as repeat mentors for new proteges, year after year. For example, veteran mentors report satisfaction from "giving back" to an organization that has been good to them for over 30 years on average (I learned that true "rails" who have "railroading in their blood" tend to be long-term employees). I've heard these veteran mentors half-jokingly tell their proteges "I'm here to ensure your development because this will ensure your pension – and mine." No wonder these proteges get such sound career guidance to take on more responsible tasks and positions, including transitioning from Labor into Management with their union's blessing.

## 9. Mentor and protege benefits:

Research on *informal* mentoring has consistently documented that the relatively few proteges who are chosen to be recipients, benefit in nearly every way compared to their non-mentored peers. For example, if the proteges were mentored during their university studies, they get better initial jobs, at more prestigious companies or universities upon graduation, where their careers advance faster and they more quickly receive a higher salary than non-mentored peers. If mentored proteges gain employment within a university, they get more grants funded, and more articles and books published, which earns them faster tenure and promotion.

These benefits occur because mentors intentionally assisted *career advancement* for their proteges by being (a) Advocates who spoke favorably about their proteges to enhance their reputations and (b) Sponsors who recommended their proteges for special assignments that showcased the protege's particular talents.

In contrast, the main purpose of *formalized* mentoring for proteges is to provide an *enrichment* experience that develops each protege's talent and new competencies, *qualifies* proteges for more responsible work assignments (where their talents can be showcased), *prepares* proteges for career advancement opportunities when these become available, and increases proteges' *loyalty* to the organization so they stay (reducing costly turnover is a main reason for these programs starting). Program Guidelines prevent mentors from being Advocates or Sponsors, for this can motivate non-participating peers to undermine or sabotage the *formalized* mentoring program.

A key activity in *formalized* mentoring – worth emphasizing repeatedly – is to create and carry out an agreed upon **Mentoring Action Plan** – because completed Plans provide evidence of goal attainment and what was done to produce this. **CSX Transportation** provides one of the best examples of this. After nine years, some 20 groups had participated in CSX's *formalized* mentoring program. Doug Klippel (one of the coordinators) and I were asked to give a conference presentation about their program and the benefits it produced. Doug did a statistical analysis of the benefits reported by all the proteges and mentors who had participated. He then phoned me to say: "I have a Ph. D. in statistics and have analyzed the data repeatedly, but I cannot make sense out of the results. The mentors and the proteges who report the most benefits are in long distance relationships – they work in different locations. How are these results possible?"

I replied: "I don't know. Why don't you phone partners in the same location and in different locations to find out the answer from them?" He did, and phoned me to say: "Partners in long distant relationships made a commitment to one another to carry out the Mentoring Action Plan they created during Partner Training, so that when they talked on the phone or actually met, they were prepared for each activity they had scheduled. Partners, who saw one another frequently, did not stick to their Plan and were not as well prepared for meetings; they more often *did lunch* or *just talked.*"

The ***Mentoring Action Plan*** (MAP) was the first customized mentoring product I developed in 1978 to ensure that partners (a) agree on activities they will do together or separately, (b) they are both prepared for scheduled meetings, (c) they carry out agreed upon activities, and (d) they achieve the protege's goal for that Plan. I fully realized just how important the MAP is when I did research on grade 5 and 6 proteges, who rank-ordered "carrying out the agreed-upon Plan" as the most important of 10 activities they did with formalized mentors. This one activity accounted for .48 percent of the variance; the statistical significance of this happening by chance has a probability of *p<.0001* (which is extremely significant).

Bottom line: The ***MAP*** provides a "roadmap" for mentoring partners to follow to reach their destination (goal attainment). Each MAP converts Talk into Action Steps that produce intended Results.


## 10. How mentoring ends:

*Informal* mentoring relationships often end in a bitter power struggle because there is no designated end date that formally terminates the relationship. Sometimes the protege wants to leave the relationship, but the mentor doesn't want the protege to leave. Sometimes the mentor believes it's time for the protege to leave, but the protege doesn't want to and feels "kicked out."

This power struggle doesn't "happen" in *formalized* mentoring programs because both partners are aware when their *formalized* relationship will end. They know this from the start. So, from the beginning, the mentor equips and empowers the protege to leave the formal relationship. And the protege responds to this assistance, in preparation for leaving. Sometimes, partners will continue to meet less formally – perhaps by continuing to address the protege's identified needs in the ways described above or perhaps by "doing their own thing."

### Superior (or "Boss") as Mentor

Before you leave Chapter 1, I want to make one more important point. In 150 *formalized* mentoring programs I've helped to plan and implement, the Planning Team has seldom used Superiors (e.g., supervisors, managers, other "bosses") as mentors for their direct reports (except at the very highest levels for developing leaders) because these Superiors must *make performance evaluations* of their direct reports.

It is very awkward when the same person is both an "evaluator" and a "helper." It is difficult for the protege to bring up and discuss really sensitive issues in *confidence* with the mentor (e.g., "I don't feel my work is appreciated and properly rewarded here, so I'm thinking of leaving.") because this same person as the Superior might perceive this direct report as "having a bad attitude" and might later record this in a negative performance evaluation.

Fulfilling such contrasting dual roles – evaluator/helper and evaluated/helped – is very difficult for one person to do (superior/mentor) with another person in a complementary dual role (direct report/protege). [I rewrote this last sentence five times to clearly state what I was trying to say. If I had this much difficulty, imagine how much more difficult it is for the two people who are trying to fulfill these four roles.]

Have you ever had to fulfill the dual roles of evaluator *and* helper – or been the person evaluated *and* helped? Have you found it difficult for a superior/mentor to wear "both hats" (evaluator/helper) so that the direct report/protege felt comfortable shifting to the corresponding role (evaluated/helped) and knew when to do this?

Of the 20,000 proteges who have participated in *formalized* mentoring programs I helped to create, only a few said: "I want my manager (or "boss") to be my mentor. Most proteges said: "I want a confidant." "I can get help for normal issues from my manager, but not for confidential issues." "My boss won't support what I really want to do."

**Summarized Tips for Mentors & Proteges:**
1. Emphasize both *Career* and *Psychosocial* assistance for proteges.
2. Find out how to progress to *become* an **EXPERT** in a dedicated field. [See Stages for becoming an EXPERT in the table below.]
3. Avoid implementing *informal* mentoring practices that can lead to Failure.
4. Don't expect *formalized* mentoring to produce the same results that *informal* mentoring produces over a much longer time (5-8 years or more).
5. Mentors: avoid mentoring your direct reports – unless absolutely necessary.
6. Proteges: avoid being mentored by a Superior/Boss – unless absolutely necessary.

**Summarized Tips for Coordinators & Mentoring Champions:**
1. To prevent problems exclude *Advocate* and *Sponsor* as Mentor Roles.
2. Ensure mentors provide both *Career* and *Psychosocial* assistance.
3. Do not make simple "***Announcements***" or implement partially planned "***Initiatives***." Instead, have a proven **EXPERT** develop a *formalized*

mentoring "***Program***" where all essential components are defined, designed and delivered.

4. Never match Experts with Novices as mentoring partners (this won't work).

5. Understand the 10 main characteristics of *informal* mentoring and don't incorporate these into your *formalized* mentoring program.

6. Don't expect the same results from a shorter *formalized* program that *informal* mentoring produces over many years.

7. Above all, remember that you are the ***single most important person*** in a successful *formalized* mentoring program, and thus must be *involved in all aspects of it.*

| Level | Main Characteristics of an EXPERT in developing appropriate *Formalized* Mentoring Programs |
|---|---|
| *Expert* | Has at least 10 dedicated years developing distinctive mentoring programs (for new hires, career development, new leaders, etc.). Experience is broad and deep.<br><br>Intuitively aware of important variables in any new situation. Able to use different paradigms and heuristics to solve problems quickly and creatively.<br><br>As a *Reflective Practitioner* self-assesses what works and doesn't. Engages in "forward" reasoning to solve a problem.<br><br>Aligns right processes to produce *multiple outcomes* (for diversified workforce + explore career path options + develop needed competencies + reduce turnover when advancement not possible).<br><br>Develops the *Guiding Principles* that lower Levels follow. |
| *Proficient* | Has at least 5 years of varied experiences. Employs *Guiding Principles* from Experts.<br><br>Becoming a *Reflective Practitioner* (see Level above). Can plan and implement several *different types* of mentoring programs, each of which produces a desired outcome. |
| *Competent* | Has repeated experience doing the same thing. (e.g., can plan and implement one type of mentoring program – such as for orienting new hires better, but not for developing leadership competencies). |
| *Advanced Beginner* | Knows "about" mentoring, but has limited practical know-how. Can partially plan a mentoring "Initiative" – but not a fully planned *formalized* program that produces intended outcomes. |
| *Novice* | May have gathered information, read books or articles, but lacks understanding based on experience. Has "head |

<table>
<tr><td></td><td>knowledge" without "practical know-how." Makes simplistic "Announcements" to encourage "do-your-own-thing" mentoring (lacks planning).</td></tr>
</table>

The 5-level model above is based on meta-analyses of other research on what it takes to become an Expert in a dedicated field of focus. See: Dreyfus, H. and Dreyfus, S. (2005). Expertise in real world contexts, *Organization Studies*, 26(5), 779-792.

### What a Non-Expert did:

**Shell Oil** (in Miri, on the island of Borneo) hired an external consultant to create a Mentoring Scheme for 300 proteges and 300 mentors. Because goals were not defined, proteges were matched with "wrong" mentors who could not help them achieve intended goals. Program delivery consisted of training proteges and mentors separately (each group trained for a week). No coordinator was trained to ensure mentoring partners were meeting and everything was working.

Results: Shell Oil wasted over $1,000,000 because Mentoring Partners did not know HOW to engage in effective mentoring. Over 12 months, 600 participants wasted time and money, because mentoring did not enable proteges to meet their individual needs and achieve desired goals, nor did it reduce turnover or enable career exploration, as expected.

### What we did as Experts:

With input from the Mentoring Task Force and focus groups (comprised of participants), we facilitated **Collaborative Program Planning** to *define, design* and *deliver* three different types of Formalized Mentoring Programs:

- We designed an **Orientation Mentoring Program** to get newly hired university graduates up-to-speed faster. Capable peers served as mentors. Our *Protege Needs Inventory* enabled each protege to identify specific needs so that peer mentors could systematically provide needed assistance.
- We designed a **Career Expansion Mentoring Program** to reduce the costly turnover of high potentials – at a time when promotion was not possible. Mentors helped these proteges expand their technical expertise by carrying out a carefully planned, highly challenging *Mentor-Assisted Project* in the mentor's area of expertise.
- We designed a **Career Exploration Mentoring Program** to enable longer-term employees to explore and choose a career path that was best for them and for the company. Top-level technical and managerial veterans provided mentoring.

This case study and 50 others are described in my book covering 45+ years of my professional work/passion:

*Mentoring, Skill Coaching & Knowledge Solutions*
*Different Resolutions for Different Challenges*

# Chapter 7

## *Formalized* Mentoring Ends Well
## & Produces Effective Mentors

**In Chapter 7**, you'll learn to apply what you learned in preceding chapters. You'll also learn:

> ➤ How to end your mentoring partnership well – and avoid ending badly, like *informal* mentoring often ends.

> ➤ How the *6-Step Mentoring Process* produces multiple benefits.

> ➤ How a *Mentoring Partner Agreement* produces multiple benefits

> ➤ How Proteges Can Manage *Situational Mentoring* [my personal example]

You can read my poem – ***Mentor Me*** – which illustrates a protege becoming a mentor who knows how to engage in *Situational Mentoring*.


## Start Mentoring to End Well


In Chapter 6 you learned that informal mentoring develops through well-defined Stages. The last Stage can end well if the mentoring relationship is Transformed or Redefined so that mentoring partners "become colleagues or friends." BUT, this depends on what takes place in the preceding Stage:

> ❖ **Parting** usually involves a "power struggle" as the protege seeks independence (according to Linda Phillips-Jones).

> ❖ **Separation** can be hurtful as the protege seeks independence (according to Kathy Kram).


This kind of hurtful, power struggle does not occur in *formalized* mentoring relationships, because both partners know at the *beginning* that their formal relationship will *officially end* at a designated point in time. This is publicized and accepted by candidates before they are selected to participate in a formalized mentoring program. Partners can agree to continue meeting 'unofficially' – after *officially meeting* for the period they have committed to meet

Below, is Doug Klippel's testimonial about the impact of my Partner Training activities at CSX Transportation. This is followed by an actual example.

> "After 2000, I took over from Bill and conducted his Mentoring for Results Partner Training for CSX – even after I started my own company. I know from 18 years experience as a coordinator and trainer that virtual strangers (who have been matched as partners) feel so comfortable that mentoring actually occurs during partner training. Partners compare protege needs and mentor expertise after answering the Protege Needs Inventory. Partners discuss difficult challenges using Bill's 6-Step Mentoring Process – and then plan how to address this using a Mentoring Action Plan. Partners learn how to use four Mentoring Styles for giving/receiving assistance, after answering Bill's Mentoring Style Indicator.
>
> Even during two recessions, Mentoring for Results Partner Training has continued to take place because it produces **Mentoring Relationships that Produce Results!"**

> ~**Dr. Doug Klippel**, former Mentoring Coordinator at CSX and current President of People Development Partners (http://www.peopledevpartners.com)

## Examples of How *Formalized* Mentoring Ends Well

### 1. *6-Step Mentoring Process*
### Produces Multiple Benefits

Below is an actual example of my 6-Step Mentoring Process. I demonstrated this while helping a 'volunteer protege' resolve a challenging situation at **CSX Transportation**. It was not scripted or rehearsed. It's what I can still recall after nearly 30 years – because of its continuing benefits for the protege and mentor, and CSX.

It started when I asked:

"Who wants to volunteer to role play being my protege? I'm looking for a volunteer with a real challenge, which you cannot resolve on your own, which you are willing to share with everyone here. We cannot keep this confidential just between you and me."

I had noticed that Jerry was the most socially outgoing, buoyant person in the room – shaking everyone's hand, sought out and hugged, constantly being asked, "How are you doing."

Because I had found out why, I asked jerry to role-play being my protege. Everyone encouraged him. Here's why.

**Step 1: Understand Protege's Needs, Goals, Attitudes and Perceptions**

I asked, "Why did you volunteer?" and Jerry told me: "My wife died of cancer two years ago, leaving me to raise two sons in high school on my own." To do this, he got transferred from traveling Salesmen ["which I love"] to doing office work ["so I don't have to leave my boys alone"].

While holding back tears, Jerry eventually revealed his challenge: "I love selling and meeting new people. I'm one of CSX's top salesmen. Now, I'm stuck at a desk, doing repetitive office work ... I hate this ... it's not me and it doesn't benefit CSX."

[This important first Step took 15 minutes and lots of empathic listening, asking clarifying questions, and encouraging Jerry to candidly share with me what everyone already knew.]

## Step 2: Help Protege Realize Actions and Consequences

I asked: "Would you tell me *what you've tried* and *how it worked*?"

I patiently waited for Jerry's reply: "I've tried to develop a positive attitude."

"I got my boss to assign a person to do routine paperwork I cannot do very well."

"Other people have stepped in whenever I need help."

"My friends and colleagues take my boys to play their sports, help with homework, cook their favorite meals."

I asked: "Has anything worked for you, Jerry?"

Looking down (overwhelmed) and depressed (no buoyancy), Jerry replied: "Nothing ... and I can't figure out any solutions. I realize I cannot keep trying to do office work I hate."

## Step 3: Identify the Protege's Real Issue

I said: "I've listened to what you've shared with me. Would you like me to say what I think your *Real Issue* is?"

After Jerry said, "Yes" I summarized what he had said in Steps 1&2: "You love selling because you are *highly creative* – you like *satisfying* your customer's needs. You love your previous lifestyle because you like *being independent* – travelling and meeting new people – and then returning home to your *family*. The real issue is *your sons* ... and what to do so they are properly cared for. This is your *number one priority* now. Is what I'm saying accurate?"

Jerry replied "Yes!" and his countenance brightened as though the proverbial light bulb lit up in his mind. "But I still don't have a clue what to do."

## Step 4: Develop Productive Goals, Attitudes and Perceptions

I said, "Let's identify your main *Goal* that we need to focus on."

Jerry's creative mind pondered, then he smiled and replied with a positive laugh that signalled his *new perception*, "I need a family to take care of my family ... my boys and me."

I confirmed this *new insight* ["You can't be as independent as you used to be"] and *positive Goal* ["You need a family to adopt you and your boys"]. Jerry laughed again.

**Step 5: Expand Protege's Thinking to Consider New Options**

I said, "Let's brainstorm possibilities," and Jerry agreed. I asked, "Is there a family that will take in you and your sons, so all three of you become part of their family?"

Jerry and I were discussing several potential families when a long-time Oversight Committee member named John interjected:

"Sorry for interrupting, but I just have to say this. I'm a senior vice-president here ... in case you don't know me. I have one more year before retiring. My family has known Jerry's family for some 20 years ... we've done many fun activities together. We have a huge house that will be empty in a few months, after our boys go off to university. I need to check with my wife and kids ... but I think they will welcome Jerry and his boys moving in. My wife will like having Jerry's boys to look after ... they're both so polite. I like spending time with Jerry ... when he's not travelling as CSX's best salesman."

**Step 6: Agree on a *Mentoring Action Plan* to Handle Protege's Situation**

Everyone was still buzzing with delight when I stopped them to say: "John, it seems your invitation to adopt Jerry and his boys will satisfy his Goal of making sure his boys are properly looked after so he can continue selling. So, let's agree on next steps."

John and Jerry agreed, and we decided on these next steps in a *Mentoring Action Plan*:

1) John gets wife's approval. If 'yes' then proceed.
2) Jerry's family dialogues with John's family to get everyone's approval. If 'yes' then proceed.
3) Jerry gets his Boss' approval to resume selling. If 'yes' then proceed.
4) Jerry rents his home to generate extra money to pay expenses living in John's home.
5) Jerry and his sons move in.
6) John and his wife take care of Jerry's boys while he travels and sells.
7) Jerry resumes selling with even greater gusto and creativity ... to become CSX's top salesmen once again.
8) Everyone lives happily ever after. [All of the observers clapped their approval. Some laughed. Some cried.]

I've role modeled **over 100 Demos**, but none is as memorable as this one with Jerry because of the very real positive impact it had on everyone involved – including CSX's revenues from Jerry's sales.

## 2. Completing a *Mentoring Action Plan*
## Ends Formalized Mentoring with a Sense of Accomplishment

The Demo above ended with the creation of a ***Mentoring Action Plan*** [MAP] that converted "Talk" that occurred during Steps 1-5 into "Action Steps" in Step 6. When this "Road MAP" was carried out to completion, everyone benefitted, including CSX.

CSX invested more money in their formalized mentoring program than any of my other 150+ clients. Completed *Mentoring Action Plans* documented what was done and learned. It is even more important to complete MAPs when mentor-protege partners are in "long-distance" relationships, as Doug Klippel explained in ENDORSEMENTS at the front of this book – and is repeated here:

> "After the first eight years, I statistically analyzed all the data from about 300 participants and found that the mentors and proteges who reported the most benefits had been in long-distance relationships (not living or working in the same state). This outcome occurred because Dr. Gray taught partners to create an Action Plan during partner training and then use this to schedule meetings and be prepared for them. The long-distance partners did this better than same-location partners.
>
> After 2000, I took over from Bill and conducted his Mentoring for Results Partner Training for CSX – even after I started my own company....
>
> Even during two recessions, Mentoring for Results Partner Training has continued to take place because it produces ***Mentoring Relationships that Produce Results!***"

> ~**Dr. Doug Klippel**, former Mentoring Coordinator at CSX and current President of People Development Partners (http://www.peopledevpartners.com)

Since the late 1970s, I've developed many customized Mentoring Materials. The first was the ***Mentoring Action Plan*** [MAP] because it produces a sense of accomplishment. Here is the story:

I fully realized just how important a ***MAP*** is when I did research on grade 5 and 6 proteges: 31 proteges rank-ordered "completing the agreed-upon Plan" as the most important of 10 Activities they did while carrying out a formalized Mentor-Assisted Enrichment Project over a 10-week period. This #1 Activity – completing the Plan – accounted for .48 percent of the variance; the statistical significance of this #1 Ranking "happening by chance" has a probability of $p<.0001$ (which is extremely significant).

In sum: these young proteges realized that "completing the agreed-upon Plan" produced a "sense of accomplishment" like none of the other nine Activities they did with formalized mentors. Here's how this occurred:

The ***Mentoring Action Plan*** (MAP) ensured that partners (a) agreed on

Activities they will do together or separately, (b) they both came prepared for scheduled meetings, (c) they carried out agreed upon activities, and (d) they completed the Plan to achieve the protege's goal for that Plan.

Bottom line: The *MAP* provides a "Road MAP" for mentoring partners to follow to reach their destination (goal attainment).

Each MAP converts *Talk* into *Action Steps* that produce intended *Results*.

### 3. *Mentoring Partner Agreement* Produces Multiple Benefits

Below is a partner activity from my ***Mentoring for Results Partner Training***.

During Partner Training – at the beginning of the relationship – a ***Mentoring Partner Agreement*** is agreed upon and signed to enhance commitment and prevent problems. An important part is agreeing on **Major Benefits** to achieve for the protege and mentor, and for the sponsoring organization. This is important because:

✓ Formalized mentoring is typically started to *benefit proteges* in ways that informal mentoring cannot.

✓ *Mentors must benefit* so they continue volunteering to mentor the next group of proteges.

✓ Their *organization must benefit* to justify the money and time spent on supporting all components of formalized mentoring – often during the workday.

---

## *Mentoring Partner Agreement*
### Agree on Expectations, Concerns & Desired Benefits

**Directions:**

1. Discuss each question with your partner, then write down agreed-upon answers to all questions.

2. Sign below to indicate your commitment to abide by these written agreements.

### A. Agree on Expectations:

1. When [how often] and where will you meet? _______________________________

2. Who will initiate meetings and interactions? _______________________________

3. If meetings are not occurring as expected , what will you do? ________________

4. On which topics of discussion will you both maintain confidentiality?

---

5. Any other expectations not mentioned above?

___________________________________________________________

**B. Agree on Concerns about Potential Problems:**
1. Are you concerned about not having enough time to get together regularly? ____
If a problem, how will you resolve it?

___________________________________________________________

2. If you feel mis-matched, how will you handle this?

___________________________________________________________

3. What will Mentor do if Protege does not ask for needed help?

___________________________________________________________

4. What will you both do if Mentor cannot provide needed help?

___________________________________________________________

5. Any other concerns not mentioned above?

___________________________________________________________

**C. Agree on Major Benefits to be Achieved Through This Relationship:**
1. Major benefits Protege desires:

___________________________________________________________

2. Major benefits Mentor desires:

___________________________________________________________

3. Major benefits your Organization desires:

___________________________________________________________

**Our signatures indicate our commitment to abide by these recorded agreements:**
   **Mentor's signature & date:**
   **Protege's signature & date:**
©William A. Gray 1984

---

### 4. "Silo Busting" at CSX Transportation
### Produced Multiple Benefits

In the early 1990s, **CSX Transportation** started its **Associate Development Program** (ADP) to become more competitive, serve customers better, and increase profitability.

CSX hired me to conduct *Mentoring for Results Partner Training* for CSX personnel at all levels. The overarching purpose was to "break down Silos" existing between management and the union, and between departments.

To foster "Silo Busting," I encouraged mentoring partners in different functions (e.g., sales and finance) to engage in **reciprocal mentoring** to break down silo thinking and gain a better appreciation of each other's contributions to the overall company.

Over an eight year period, some 300 mentoring partners signed the **Mentoring Partner Agreement** illustrated above. Below is a description of how two proteges and their mentors – and CSX Transportation – benefitted from engaging in formalized mentoring. [This was recorded in ADP's 1996 Commemorative Booklet.]

## How Proteges Can Manage *Situational Mentoring*

**[my personal transformation & transition]**

After teaching and doing research for 15 years as a tenured professor at UBC (University of British Columbia), my wife (Marilynne) and I left academia to make a **career transition**: from salaried academics to entrepreneurs who generated our own income. We wanted to start a full-time business that focused on helping organizations define, design and deliver successful *formalized* mentoring programs for different kinds of proteges and purposes.

Before leaving UBC in January of 1986, I sought out mentor assistance to make this *transition*. Little did I know this would require a *transformation* in my thinking and actions.

I asked several close friends who owned their own businesses to mentor me in particular ways. None knew anything about the concepts and practices described in this book, but I did. So, I used this knowledge to **manage my mentors** – to guide them – so each mentor give me the help he thought I needed (based on knowledge about me and about running their own businesses).

Ken Bailey was my first and best mentor. He gave me my first business contract and helped me plan and deliver it. He, in turn, benefited because I helped his start-up software development company (initially called **Pathfinder**, now called **StarGarden**) grow from 7 to 14 to 24 employees over two years, and save $40,000 annually by coaching customers to use their software – because of what they learned from me.

Here is how I *managed* my first mentor, Ken Bailey. Knowing he is always very busy, I needed to be well prepared for our meetings. Because I knew my **6-Step Mentoring Process** is effective and efficient, I used it to guide Ken's assistance and to request specific mentoring behaviors typically used with each Step.

I cannot provide a verbatim Transcription of the actual interaction (it was not taped) like I did for mentoring Elaine (it was taped and thus could be transcribed), so I've clustered together what I said, followed by what Ken said. [*Requested* and *provided* mentoring behaviors are *italicized* so you can easily recognize them.]

## Step 1: Mentor understands Protege's Needs, Goals, Attitudes and Perceptions.

"Ken, I have some ideas for marketing to education groups and corporations. Will you be a *sounding board* while I describe my ideas, and *clarify* anything that sounds unworkable? Will you *advise* me to correct any attitudes or perceptions that I need to change?"

Ken mostly *listened* like I requested – to find out what I wanted to do. He knew I was heavily involved in developing mentoring programs. He did *question* my ability and plan to *market* to both groups at the same time.

## Step 2: Mentor reviews Protege's Actions and Consequences.

"Ken, I'd like to describe some things I've already done and the consequences. Would you *listen* and *summarize* what you think are the key points? And ask me *probing questions* so I'll think of additional things I might do? If you think I need your *advice* or a *prescription* of exactly what to do, please tell me. If I need any *coaching*, will you provide this?" [Marilynne and I were organizing the First International Conference on Mentoring, to be held at UBC in July of 1986. I described the "contact information" we were amassing as we identified potential Presenters and Delegates from educational, corporate and government sectors.]

Ken and I *dialogued* about how I might use this contact information, and this conference, for marketing purposes. Ken provided the mentoring assistance I requested, plus other kinds he thought I needed. He also *encouraged* our self-motivation and *praised* what we had done. He *asked probing questions* to find out how I could market to both groups simultaneously.

## Step 3: Mentor identifies Protege's Real Issue.

"Ken, thus far I've been presenting and discussing what I want to do and have been doing. Did I express anything that might cause failure, like some real issue you can *clarify* for me? Do you need to point out or *confront* any incongruities or conflicts between my goals, attitudes, or perceptions? Is there any *real issue* I need to resolve?"

Ken pointed out that I avoided discussing "selling" – and had difficulty telling him my consultation fees and the prices for products I had developed and was planning to sell.

He *explained* that I was still thinking like an educator, who wants to "give away" what he knows instead of charging a fair price for this. He gave pricing *suggestions* that were helpful for both Sales and Marketing purposes.

## Step 4: Mentor helps Protege develop More Productive Goals, Attitudes, and Perceptions.

"Ken, do I need to re-define my goals or attitudes or perceptions related to marketing – or to selling? If I do, would you *self-disclose* what you did and *describe* what other people did – what worked and didn't? It's okay to *persuade* me to do what you think I should do, if you think I need a push because I'm stuck on my own ideas. You might *ask questions* that force me to think or act differently. If I say anything you agree with, please *encourage* this so I know I'm on the right track. And *clarify* anything I say."

Ken immediately *clarified* my obvious confusion about Marketing and Sales – *explaining* how they are related, but different. Again, he *asked questions* about which group – education or corporations – I planned to focus on, and *encouraged* our efforts to attract 300 or more potential Conference Delegates, with about 50% coming from each group.

**Step 5: Mentor expands Protege's Thinking to Consider New Options.**

"Ken, I probably need to think of new marketing options. Will you *self-disclose* marketing tips that work for you – and what hasn't worked? Can you *teach* me a crash course on marketing? Is there anything else that can help me – your *suggestions* or *arranging other assistance*?

Ken systematically *taught* the main functions and purposes of Marketing and Sales that he had previously *explained*. He shared "lessons learned" by *self-disclosing* some of his own marketing successes and failures. He *suggested* I hire an experienced sales person. We *discussed* ideas for marketing to Delegates immediately after the Conference.

**Step 6: Mentor and Protege agree on and commit to Carry Out a Workable Action Plan to achieve the redefined Protege Goal.**

"Ken, we've talked about so many things – ideas, possibilities, changes I need to make. I'm feeling overwhelmed. So, let's *decide together* those action steps I should put into an *agreed-upon Plan* to carry out for Marketing. I want to get maximum value from underwriting the total cost of the Conference. Marilynne and I will be giving several high-profile presentations that will showcase what we can do, so I'd also like to capitalize on this. What *advice* can you give me? Have I said anything that you need to *clarify*, so it will work better?"

Ken *summarized* the best things we previously discussed; we *jointly decided* which things could be action steps to carry out; we *agreed* on these actions and put them into a Marketing Plan I would carry out.

Again, Ken *advised* me to choose either education or corporations to target – and to think like a businessman who charges a fair price for providing knowledge and products.

Because I had not totally reached the *Consciously Competent Level* for successful Marketing or Sales, I did not heed Ken's advice immediately and thus attempted to market to both groups for the first two years.

During this period, I documented that we spent 80% of our time, effort and money marketing to **education** groups because of our backgrounds as educators, but got only 20% of our sales revenues from education groups. That's when we switched our marketing and selling focus to corporations, which furnished 80% of our revenues from 20% of our effort, time and money.

In hindsight, I should have heeded Ken's wisdom sooner: choose either education or corporations as initial clients to target. My company – Mentoring Solutions – would have become successful sooner.

#####

## Formalized Mentoring Develops Mentors who can provide Situational Mentoring

A major shortcoming of "doing-your-own-thing" during *informal* mentoring is that such 'unstructured' mentoring  is difficult to 'pass on' to others who want to provide mentoring after benefitting as a protege.

In contrast to this, the kind of formalized mentoring described throughout this book provides a 'structured template' of how to provide mentoring to proteges.

For example:
At Winthrop Pharmaceuticals, we decided that Future Leaders (proteges) would rotate every six months – over 36 months – to another C-Level mentor (CEO, CTO, CFO, COO, etc.) to gain new perspectives and leadership competencies from each mentor. We trained the first  group of mentor-protege partners to learn and apply what you've learned in this book. When proteges were matched with their next mentors, training was reduced because mentors already knew what to do. [After this 36-month formalized mentoring program ended, proteges became mentors to another group of future leaders – applying what they had been trained to do.]

To conclude this book, let me summarize in a poem – *Mentor Me ... Let Me Mentor You* – much of what you've read. My poem illustrates a protege becoming a mentor who knows how to engage in *Situational Mentoring* like that provided for this protege.

### *Mentor Me ... Let Me Mentor You*
#### © William A. Gray 1992-2023

You've been there ... where I want to go,
Equip me to succeed ... by sharing what you know.
And, when I choose a different road ... the one less taken,
Empower my initiative ... and my passion.
Mentor me!

Impart your wisdom ... when I know not what to do,

Self-disclose hard lessons ... your life experience has taught you,
Explain the unwritten rules ... the do's and the don'ts,
Inform me and guide me ... as you teach me the ropes.
Mentor me ... with what you know!

Suggest options to consider ... when one method does not matter,
Give me strong advice ... when failure must be avoided,
Prescribe a game plan ... when there's one best course to follow,
Equip me for each and every different occasion I encounter.
Mentor me ... situationally!

Be my sounding board ... take the time to listen,
Clarify my ideas ... without being judgmental,
Understand my real concerns ... identify underlying issues,
Dialogue and problem-solve ... and make decisions together.
Mentor me ... to function proactively!

Confront my inconsistencies ... when I'm unaware of them,
Persuade me to take action ... when action must be taken.
Role model your practical know-how ... that works for you,
Coach the skills I need ... to enhance performance and results.
Mentor me ... realistically!

Encourage my creativity ... and my passion to set sail,
Protect me from unfair criticism ... when I try but fail.
Praise my successes ... bless my long-held dreams,
Equip and empower me ... depending on my needs.
Mentor me ... appropriately!

As I gain in confidence ... with each new thing I do,
And become more conscious ... being aware of what to do.
And develop new competencies ... being more able,
And I stretch and grow ... becoming ever more capable,
Let me ... mentor you!

**Summarized Tips for Mentors & Proteges:**
1. Be aware of how a hurtful, power struggle can end your relationship badly – and agree to prevent this.
2. Proteges can identify a challenging situation and *manage your mentor* to employ Mentoring Style Flexibility while using the 6-Step Mentoring Process to help you handle it successfully – like I did with Ken Bailey.
3. Apply what you've learned to do as a mentor, by mentoring others.

**Summarized Tips for Coordinators & Mentoring Champions:**
1. Explain how a hurtful, power struggle can end *informal* mentoring relationships badly. Foster ending well by publicizing a Start and End date

for *formalized* mentoring.

2. Monitor relationships to make sure partners are satisfied. If not, help them work together more compatibly. If they cannot, re-match to a more compatible partner – so this relationship will end well.

**Keep reading ....**

If you want to learn more about my avocation for mentoring and 45+ years vocation – from Pioneer in this field in 1978 to Expert today.

My book describes 45+ years of my work/passion:

# *Mentoring, Skill Coaching & Knowledge Solutions*
### *Different Resolutions for Different Challenges*

**by**
**William A. Gray, Ph.D.**

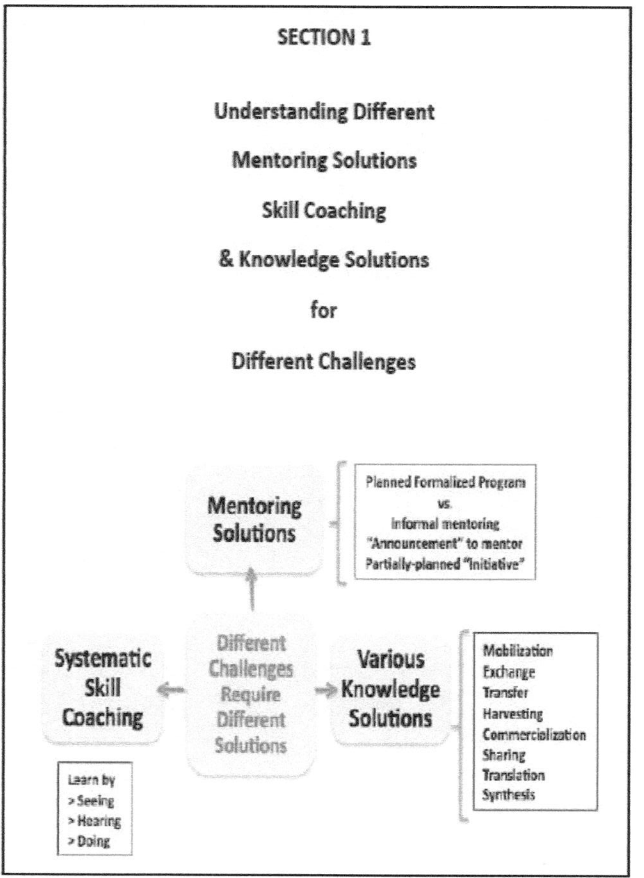

SECTION 1
Understanding Different
Mentoring Solutions
Skill Coaching
& Knowledge Solutions
for
Different Challenges
Mentoring Solutions
Planned Formalized Program
vs.
Informal mentoring
"Announcement" to mentor
Partially-planned "Initiative"
Systematic Skill Coaching
Different Challenges Require Different Solutions
Various Knowledge Solutions
Mobilization
Exchange
Transfer
Harvesting
Commercialization
Sharing
Translation
Synthesis
Learn by
> Seeing
> Hearing
> Doing


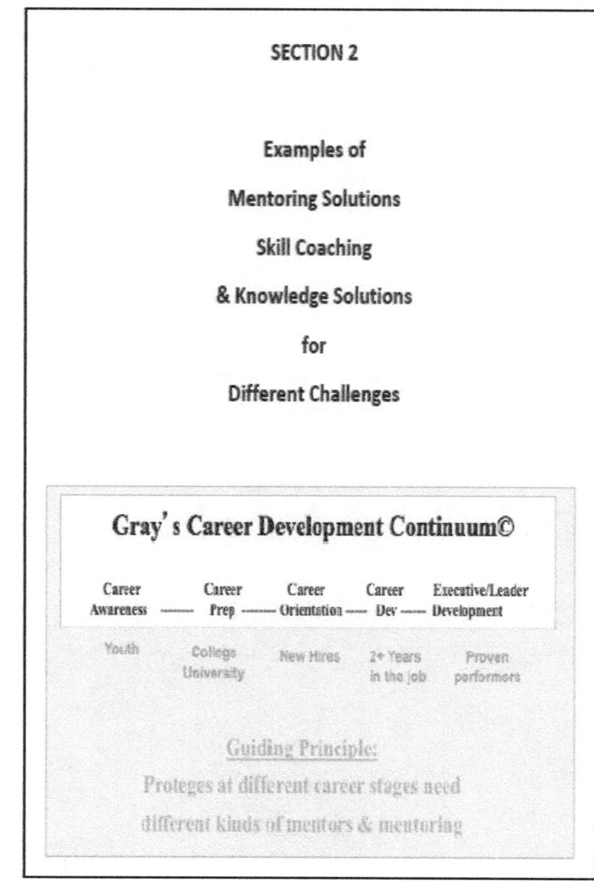

SECTION 2
Examples of
Mentoring Solutions
Skill Coaching
& Knowledge Solutions
for
Different Challenges
Gray's Career Development Continuum©
Career Awareness — Career Prep — Career Orientation — Career Dev — Executive/Leader Development
Youth
College University
New Hires
2+ Years in the job
Proven performers
Guiding Principle:
Proteges at different career stages need
different kinds of mentors & mentoring

# ABOUT THE AUTHOR

## William A. Gray, Ph.D.

### President of Mentoring Solutions®

While I was a professor at the University of British Columbia, I first began developing formalized mentoring programs and researching essential components so that this became my avocation and then my vocation for 45+ years.

Seeing the benefits that collaboratively planned mentoring programs produced for proteges, mentors and the sponsoring organization, I left academia in 1986 to devote myself full-time to developing mentoring programs [along with my wife and business partner, Marilynne Miles Gray]. Together, we organized and sponsored the First International Conference on Mentoring (held in Vancouver, July 1986), and for the next six years published the only journal on mentoring – called *Mentoring International*.

I have trained over 20,000 mentor-protege partners to work together and produce intentional benefits, using Gray's Mentor-Protege Relationship Model™ and materials we especially developed. Such as the *Mentoring Style Indicator, Mentoring Action Plan, Mentoring Agreement,* and *Protege Needs Inventory.* Over 150 organizations have asked me to help them custom develop different kinds of mentoring programs for a wide variety of proteges and purposes; these organizations include companies, government agencies, colleges and universities, and school systems.

**Email:** wgray@mentoring-solutions.com

Visit our **website**: http://www.mentoring-solutions.com

9 798215 575840